ENOCH

A Bigfoot Story

ISBN 145154992X
ISBN 978-1-4515499-2-8

Copyright © 2010 Autumn Williams

All rights reserved. No part of this publication may be reproduced, stored in a retrieval system or transmitted, in any form or by any means, electronic, mechanical, photocopying, recording, or otherwise, without the prior written permission of the author.

Cover design: Autumn Williams
Front cover illustration: Autumn Williams
Back cover illustration: Scott Davis

ENOCH
A Bigfoot Story

AUTUMN WILLIAMS

DEDICATION

To those who have seen something
tall, hairy and wondrous.
You are not alone.

ACKNOWLEDGEMENTS

I would like to express my appreciation to those who helped make this book a reality. Without your love and support, it would never have come to be. Many heartfelt thanks…

To my mother, Sali Sheppard-Wolford, for teaching me that there are things in this world that we don't know that are *worth* knowing.

To Scott Davis, for being my rock. Always.

To Bill and Lori Hodgson, who know the true meaning of friendship and never let me forget it.

To those who make up the Oregon Bigfoot members' community.

To all of the witnesses who have bravely come forward to share their stories with others.

To the many researchers whom I count as friends.

And last, but certainly most of all, to Mike. Your story, and our friendship, has changed my life in ways I cannot express. I will always be grateful for your trust in me. Thank you, Snapperhead.

CONTENTS:

Author's forward 9

CHAPTERS:

1	BIGFOOT IN THE BACKYARD	14
2	MYSTERIOUS ENCOUNTERS	21
3	PROOF & PICTURES	28
4	TRUST	41
5	WINNING THE LOTTERY	52
6	TWO-DIMENSIONAL SASQUATCH	65
7	MEETING THE LOCALS	71
8	SURVIVAL OF THE FITTEST	87
9	THE NATURE OF THE BEAST	100
10	NOT JUST A PRETTY FACE	113
11	SKUNK APE POO	122
12	RETURN TO THE SWAMP	133
13	FEELING WATCHED	143
14	THE RENDEZVOUS	154
15	SHELBY	180
16	RESPECT	188
17	UNIQUE INSIGHT	194
18	TESTING THE WATERS	213
19	THE HUMAN ELEMENT	222
20	"PROFESSIONAL SUICIDE"	232
21	WHAT IS A SASQUATCH?	246
22	FINAL THOUGHTS	263

APPENDIX:

Tips and Cautions for Long-Term Witnesses 270

"There is a principle which is proof against all information, which is proof against all arguments, which cannot fail to keep a man in everlasting ignorance; that principle is contempt, prior to investigation."

Herbert Spencer

AUTHOR'S FORWARD

I've been asked many times why I haven't written a book about Bigfoot. I suppose I didn't feel that I had a good enough reason. Until now.

Writing a book simply to add the title of "published author" to a list of accomplishments didn't interest me. Having spent twenty of my thirty-six years on this little blue marble researching hairy hominids, it wasn't that I didn't feel I'd accumulated enough information about the subject to fill a book... or several. But what purpose, exactly, would it serve? Who would be my audience? Why spend all the time and energy if I couldn't say what I really wanted to say and make a difference in some small way? What, exactly, would I say?

Would I write about the subject of Bigfoot in general? That's been done, and done to death: the same historical references and classic stories and data and suppositions rehashed and regurgitated for your reading pleasure; the same theories mulled over by authors who attempt objectivity by never favoring one idea over another; chapters of dry facts about height, weight and hair color; detailed examinations of road-crossing sightings by witnesses who, no matter how many times you interview them, can only tell you what a Bigfoot looks like crossing the road.

These things might give those who haven't had a sighting an idea what a Bigfoot looks like, how it walks, of its size and proportions; and enough data, presented in that fashion, might convince some skeptics that Sasquatches may actually exist... but none of it truly tells us what a Bigfoot *is*. What does it eat? How does it behave? How does it interact with others of its kind? Are they compassionate? Intelligent? How would they interact with us, if we could only get close enough? What *are* they? *And why is it important?*

I suppose the goal of this book – and the difference between it and most others on the subject - is to answer those questions. The question, "Does Bigfoot exist?" has been addressed time and time again. Let's move beyond that. For just a moment, let's assume that they do.

If so, what is the nature of a Sasquatch?

This question has been the focus of my research for two decades.

I had a sighting as a child, and it probably changed my life. I doubt I would have spent my adult life concerning myself with a subject as strange as this had I not.

As the child of a family of long-term-witnesses (a phrase I coined many years ago to differentiate between those who have ongoing encounters and those incidental witnesses who simply have a single, brief sighting), I have spent the majority of my time focusing on folks who claim to live with Bigfoot in their backyards. Over the years, I've spent many long hours reviewing these encounters, interviewing eyewitnesses, and following up with them on site. As a result, I've had several encounters of my own, though not another face-to-face, up-close sighting... yet.

I could have written a book about all of that, I guess. But while I felt that I was asking the right questions, I didn't feel that any one witness had gotten close enough or experienced quite enough to provide the answers. And while I'd come to some tentative conclusions about what these things might be, the ideal context in which to relate these ideas, and why I feel it's important that we understand them, was as elusive as the creatures themselves.

Until now.

Unlike most books on this subject, a single witness' experiences, and the affect his sharing has had on my journey, will be the focus here.

When he first contacted me, I had no idea what I was in for. I don't think he did either.

He had never worked with a "Bigfoot researcher", and I had never worked with a witness who'd claimed the level of experiences he did. Several months and hundreds of hours on the phone later, I found that we had formed a friendship that took our roles beyond those of witness and researcher. I had come to like him, respect him and value him as a friend.

As he began to trust me and open up about his experiences, I found that the details he shared clarified my understanding of these creatures. Fragmented clues gleaned from interviewing other eyewitnesses and carefully reading sighting reports over the years suddenly fell into context as he unraveled parts of the mystery for me, through detailed accounts of his unique and extraordinary relationship with a species most of us are lucky to encounter even once in a lifetime.

Interestingly, the more he shared, the more I began to recognize that *our* tentative relationship and the trust that he and I were building were a synonymous reflection of the delicate relationship that he had developed with these creatures out there in the swamp. The challenges of getting to know him and building a trusting relationship weren't much different than those he described facing with his wild friends. I found the parallels amusing and sometimes frustrating – but more than that, I understood his desire to protect that relationship that he had come to cherish. I felt the same about ours and when I said I would protect his identity and the location of his encounters, I meant it.

This book is about trust.

It's about the witness trusting me enough to allow me to share with you some of his experiences and the knowledge that he has gained, trusting that I will do so without exploiting him or the creatures that he has come to know and care for. It's about my trusting the veracity of his claims to the extent that I am willing to put my credibility on the line in order to share them with you. It's about you, the reader, trusting that I've gained enough experience working with eyewitnesses to carefully determine when someone is being truthful or pulling my leg. It's about me trusting in my own ability to write clearly enough to share the context of this profound experience with you. And it's about trusting that you'll understand and respect what you read here.

Throughout my stint as a "Bigfoot researcher", my primary goal has been twofold: to share with others what I'm learning about Bigfoot while doing everything in my power to protect these creatures from harm or harassment. In other words, to study them without compromising the safety of that which I am studying. To educate without exploiting. Providing information while protecting the individuals involved in those encounters – hairy and human alike - has always left me walking a very fine line.

Most people with an interest in Bigfoot will find themselves, at least once in their lives, tromping through the wilderness, hoping for a sighting. Many will actively seek. Some may even be successful.

Every time one of us little hairless creatures encounters one of those big hairy creatures, we act as an ambassador of sorts from our species to theirs.

By writing this book, it is my hope that you will come to understand these magnificently intelligent and wonderful beings as I have; that you will feel the awe and respect for them that I do. And that you will remember, should you happen upon a Sasquatch in the woods or a Skunk Ape in the swamp, that each of us is a reflection of all of us… and please interact accordingly.

–1–

BIGFOOT IN THE BACKYARD

In the late 1970's, my family lived in a small, tarpaper shack in the foothills of Mt. Rainier in Washington state. My parents were hippies and had wanted to "get back to the land". Mom sold her washing machine, the electric range… and the five of us, my parents and we three girls, moved into the sticks.[1]

A wood cook stove was our only source of heat. Each day, after Mom got the two older girls on the school bus and my father off to work, she and I would walk the path to the river behind the house and pick up sticks for firewood. I was a toddler, traipsing along behind Mom, singing to myself and gathering twigs.

When she stopped dead in the middle of the trail that spring morning and I ran into her, the path *my* life would take was determined in a few short moments, though I didn't know it then.

I looked up at her. She wasn't looking at me. She was looking at *them*.

Two hairy, creepy people were standing off to one side of the path. The big one was huge and brown, the smaller one a lighter shade. The big one looked at us – no, *into* us - with an unblinking stare. Big, dark, penetrating eyes that appeared more animal than human (but oh, so intelligent)

---

[1] Read the full account: Sali Sheppard-Wolford, Valley Of the Skookum: Four Years of Encounters with Bigfoot (Enumclaw, WA: Pine Winds Press, 2006)

gazed at us from beneath a heavy brow. He cocked his head.

Mom muttered, "Autumn, turn around and walk… *don't run…*" out of the side of her mouth as she grabbed my hand and turned us toward the cabin. I remember thinking *Mom, you're walking too fast… I have to run* as she propelled us back along the trail to the cabin.

I wasn't afraid… at least not until I saw her reaction. The Big Guy didn't look much different from my dad and all of his longhaired, bearded hippie friends. I didn't understand then what we had seen, what those things were. It would come to haunt me.

Months later, at the B&I in Tacoma, I was lifted up to peer through the filthy glass of a tiny enclosure to see Ivan the Gorilla, the department store's star attraction. As I watched the bored, depressed animal before me, I felt compassion and a deep sadness. I asked Mom why he wasn't in the backyard with the other ones.

Looking back now, I realize that as a small child I wasn't capable of discerning the difference between hippie humans, a gorilla on display in a department store… and Sasquatches in the backyard. Young children aren't capable of incredulity. To a toddler – even a bright and inquisitive one – just about every experience is new and I didn't have any frame of reference for understanding that some things aren't "supposed" to exist.

The sightings, encounters and subtle interactions continued for my family and neighbors as we lived our lives in the forest by the Carbon River. There began a game of cat-and-mouse with these creatures – though who was the cat and who was the mouse was never quite clear. Bigfoot was a regular topic of conversation among the adults in the valley and I, a perceptive little pitcher with big ears, overheard them discussing the topic more times than I could count. As a result, "Bigfoot" was just something that *was*.

By the time I was old enough to truly understand our family's experiences, they were long over; we'd moved to Oregon and Bigfoot was no longer in our back yard. But I had developed an insatiable curiosity for things big and hairy. In elementary school, I checked out every book available on the subject, in spite of the strange looks of the teachers, librarians and bookmobile drivers. I was hooked. The other children in school tolerated my interest and excitement with mild amusement (*"Autumn's talking about Bigfoot again..."*) or outright ridicule and sat through endless book reports and class presentations as I introduced them to the idea that large, hairy, creepy people walked the forests around us.

It seemed I was the only one who cared.

Though the subject was always in the back of my mind during my forays into the woods with childhood friends, I didn't truly begin field research until the age of 16. My first index-card catalogue of sightings grew too heavy to comfortably lift. My first car, a 1968 Rambler American, endured thousands of miles of abuse as I traveled the logging roads in Douglas County, Oregon, searching for footprints, hoping to catch another glimpse of one of those forest people. I discovered the freedom and excitement of road trips and every dime I could scrape together was spent venturing back to the family homestead on the river in Washington or to the wilds of Northern California, trying to find the location of the 1967 Patterson/Gimlin film, or visiting and interviewing eyewitnesses.

The focus of my research was, naturally, those witnesses who claimed to have Bigfoot in their backyards. While few if any of the Bigfoot books I'd read detailed encounters like these, I assumed that if my family had experienced ongoing interactions with these creatures while living in a wooded rural setting, there must be others with similar experiences. And I was right. While other researchers were gathering endless reports of road crossings or frightened campers, hikers and hunters, I was interviewing folks who, like my family, had experienced ongoing interactions at home. It was then that I began to understand the differences between long-term witnesses and incidental witnesses.

These long-term witnesses were able to relate subtle behavioral details – like Bigfoot observing humans, exchanging "gifts", vocalizing, and interacting with pets and livestock, among other things – that were eerily similar to what we'd experienced in the river valley when I was a child. It struck me then that no matter how many witnesses I interviewed who'd seen a Bigfoot cross the road, and no matter how thoroughly I interviewed them, they would only be able to tell me *what a Bigfoot looks like while crossing the road*. I already knew what a Sasquatch looked like; I'd seen two of them as a child. I wanted to know what they *are*.

In the late 1990's, I discovered the internet and joined an email ListServ. In those days, the internet was still in its relative infancy; there weren't yet hundreds of Bigfoot websites and Bigfoot organizations, each with its own clever acronym. The IVBC, or Internet Virtual Bigfoot Conference, boasted some heavyweight names in Bigfoot research, including those whose books I'd grown up reading, like John Green and Peter Byrne. I was thrilled to be in the presence of such notable figures who shared my passion.

Innocently, I began posting about my own research into long-term witness cases… and was immediately informed by several list members that people who claimed to have Bigfoot in their backyards, or claimed ongoing encounters, were either certifiable, lying… or both.

I suddenly realized why I'd never noticed encounters like those of my family in all the books I'd read growing up. It wasn't that they weren't occurring. Researchers apparently weren't comfortable with the idea that Sasquatches might seek to interact with *us*.

In an attempt to make some sense out of it all, I gathered every report for the state of Oregon that I could find and learned how to write a database in order to organize the data. I spent months creating a sophisticated, detailed database and entering the information from each report. I was looking for something; I didn't know what. Some sort of pattern, perhaps - a clue to indicate when and where a Sasquatch sighting might be more likely to occur. An understanding of their nature. Something. Anything.

I didn't find it. What I did find was reports from one source corroborating independent reports from another. A light-colored Bigfoot would be sighted in a location around a particular time, according to one source, and a completely different source would document another sighting of a similar creature in the same locale, during the same month. I was fascinated and wanted to share the information, hoping that it would encourage others to submit their reports, to fill in the blanks… and that the answer would be in there somewhere, eventually. I uploaded the database to the web. OregonBigfoot.com was born… and new reports began flooding in.

While I continued to haunt the IVBC mailing list and the increasing number of Bigfoot websites that sprung up like mushrooms on a virtual forest floor, I visited them only to gather reports and eyewitness encounters. None of these "experts" seemed to have the answers I was seeking. What's more, they didn't even appear to be asking the same questions I was. (And I'd be damned if I could find a single one of them who'd even claimed to have *seen* a Sasquatch!)

To my dismay, I realized there was little that I could learn from researchers who'd been doing the same things for decades and had gotten nowhere. They would consistently disregard the notion that long-term witnesses really might possess a more intimate knowledge of these creatures than they did. Over the ensuing years, I felt plagued by frustration and loneliness as seemingly the sole researcher who was paying attention to these witnesses.

More often than not, I ended up working alone.

In the last few years, a handful of researchers have finally begun to pay attention to long-term witnesses. But still, many researchers maintain that habituators, as they're now called, are nothing more than crackpots with too much imagination and too little evidence.

Extraordinary claims require extraordinary proof. I suppose gift exchanges do seem a bit extraordinary if you're convinced that Bigfoot is a big, dumb monkey.

Bigfoot research is a "fringe" field of study. There are no degrees available in Cryptozoology, the study of hidden animals. It is not recognized as an official field of scientific pursuit. Bigfoot is an as-yet undiscovered species and we are all laypersons in this field. Not that you'd know it from all the posturing, ego, arrogance and expertise claimed by many researchers, most of whom have never laid eyes on a Sasquatch.

Having been a witness myself, I understand all too well how it feels to have self-proclaimed "experts" pronounce with certainty that Bigfoot is nothing more than a bipedal gorilla – a "North American Ape" that happens to walk upright - when what I saw with my very own eyes was *no simple ape.*

I know only one person whom I consider something of an expert on Bigfoot, though he repeatedly reminds me, "I ain't no expert."

He is not a researcher. He prefers, even, not to be referred to as a witness.

He is the friend of a wild man… and he calls him Enoch.

-2-

MYSTERIOUS ENCOUNTERS

It's April 2003 and I am somewhere in Florida. For a Pacific Northwest girl who's accustomed to cool spring rains dripping through lush forests of Douglas fir, I don't know what to make of "springtime" here. It is muggy and mucky. The air is still and *hot*. My lungs feel ready to burst and I long for a breeze. Sweat drips. Mosquitoes buzz my ears relentlessly. My knees have never felt so vulnerable as I lace up my snake boots and wonder how high a cottonmouth can strike. I've never seen an alligator in the wild and don't want to. But never mind all that. It's time to film the first sequence. I haven't been on TV before, except for that stupid commercial I got talked into doing when I worked at my local FOX affiliate. How will I know what to do? Doug, the producer for the series we're filming, calls me over.

    The "backpack" cam is lifted onto my shoulders. It's heavy - too heavy for a woman my size. I can already feel my shoulders knotting up. Didn't anyone try this thing on beforehand? A long, thin pipe with a bracket at the end holds a camera near my face. I feel stared at. Jay, the baby-faced cameraman, tugs and yanks at the backpack, almost knocking me over. He flips a switch, and the camera glows slightly red. Infrared. Doug gives him commands, checks the image. I'm just a thing. A prop. He pulls the Sony camera out of the backpack, flips open the viewfinder and shows me. My face looks funny, tinted green, eyes glowing strangely. My nose is closer to the camera than anything else is and it looks too big, my sadly deviated septum taking center stage. I make a face and he puts the recording unit away, zips me up, pats me twice. "You're ready to go, Princess." I make another face at him. I don't like being called Princess.

"Okay, good," the producer/director/soon-to-be bane of my existence says. "We're going to film a quick sequence here. Jay will follow you with the camera as you walk out into the swamp. He'll stop, and I want you to keep walking by yourself, looking around." *Okay*, I think. *I can do that*.

"Then, on your way back, I want you to run. Like something is chasing you. Breathe heavily. Got that?"

I look at him. He's got to be kidding.

"Doug, I'm a researcher. Why would I run from something I'm looking for?"

He murmurs something about needing shots for the opening of the show and sends me into the swamp.

That should have been my first clue that this show, this "documentary series" that I'd signed a contract to host, wasn't all it was cracked up to be.

Several states later, I'd been on the road for nearly nine months off and on with a crew of up to ten guys at a time. I'd never experienced so much secondhand flatulence in my life. ("Gasquatch!" was a running joke on set.) Sixteen-hour shooting days and a producer who refused to sleep made life a living hell. I sat down to figure out whether it was worth it financially and was astonished to conclude that I would have made more per hour babysitting someone's kid. I was exhausted and ready to quit. But I couldn't. I'd signed a contract and I couldn't afford a lawyer. As a result, I ended up the front-woman for a show that I felt was sensationalized and sadly lacked in any real attempt to conduct serious research.

When the series finally began to air, I cringed, finding myself the poster-child for everything that was *wrong* with Bigfoot research. Feedback on public forums was brutal. "They never stay around long enough to really investigate anything," the critics said. "Why does she always run away scared?" my peers asked. "How many times do we have to look up her nose?" I wondered the same thing. But then, I was just doing what I was told. Sign a contract, sell your soul.

Ultimately, however, the show had a positive impact on public awareness of the Bigfoot phenomenon despite the sensationalism and "docu-drama" format. Eyewitnesses began contacting me to tell their stories; they'd felt validated seeing other witnesses come forward. People who never had much of an interest in the subject stopped their channel surfing long enough to watch the silly blonde girl chasing hairy things through the woods. The first-ever television series about Bigfoot, Mysterious Encounters, was number one on the Outdoor Life Network's prime-time lineup. It was a hit.

The executive producer called me, excited because the network wanted me to sign for a second season. He asked if I had any suggestions to improve the show. I said, "Yeah. Make it an hour-long show. Half an hour's too short. Stay in one place longer. You can't hope to do any real research if you're only on location for three days. And find another host. I quit."

After a time, the re-runs stopped airing, which was fine. I couldn't stand to watch the show anyway. The grumbling in the research community died down. But I discovered that "Autumn Williams" had become a household name… at least in Bigfoot research.

Apparently, "celebrity" somehow instantly equates to "credibility". Suddenly, people were listening simply because I had appeared in their living rooms on their television screens.

I wasn't about to look a gift horse in the mouth. I decided to try to turn my disappointment with the show into something positive.

This newfound though reluctant "celebrity" status (such as it was) became a platform from which to educate the public about this phenomenon – to try to remove some of the tongue-in-cheek, mass media, sensationalistic stigma attached to the word "Bigfoot". Reports poured in to OregonBigfoot.com from all over the country, many from long-term witnesses. I soon revamped the database to include nationwide sightings. Once the "no compete" clause in my contract had run out, I spent months producing and filming a documentary to attempt to share the subject in a serious fashion with a broader audience, using all of the things I'd learned while filming the TV show. I spent another six months editing it.

The first part of the documentary received positive reviews. I had intended to complete a series of documentary films – and Part 1 should have been subtitled: *"How NOT to Conduct Bigfoot Research"*. Technology was not how the answer would come, and I knew that. But I felt it was necessary to demonstrate the fact. In subsequent episodes, I would delve deeply into what I felt *would* work, working closely with long-term witnesses. Unfortunately, the plan went awry with the birth of my daughter, and so the context of Part 1 was lost. (Part 2 was still in the can when my daughter was born, and it sits there to this day.)

About a year ago, I sat back, took stock... and felt discouraged. Despite all of the time I'd spent interviewing eyewitnesses, conducting field research, the hundreds of hours I'd put into the website, the show, the documentary... I still hadn't accomplished what I'd set out to do. *I still didn't know what Bigfoot was.*

So now what? Time spent in the field was getting me nowhere. Long-term witnesses weren't telling me anything new. I had suspicions about the nature of Bigfoot. I thought I knew what made them tick, how they might behave in a given situation, how a Sasquatch might react to this or that. But there were pieces of the puzzle that weren't fitting into place, and no one seemed to be willing or able to show me the box top. The big picture.

Until I met Mike.

Mike is a 50-year old heavy-equipment operator from Florida who emailed me out of the blue five years after Mysterious Encounters first aired.

The funny thing is, he knew who I was long before I knew him. Apparently, he'd been watching TV, too.

The first time I saw Autumn, she was on TV doing a Bigfoot show and she came to my state. When I found out that a Bigfoot researcher was in the area, it pissed me off because I don't like Bigfoot people and I did not want them coming anywhere near my Big Guy.

What if she got wind of him and went after him? What would I do? My concern was unfounded - they only stayed a few days and were gone as quickly as they arrived.

When the program aired, I was glued to the TV. I wanted to see what a Bigfoot hunter did. Well, I found myself talking to the TV, saying things like, "Hey, girlie, I tried that and it don't work. Try something else. No... That'll run them off." And that fool with her acted like he didn't want to be there in the first place. She told him to stop the car because she saw eyes, but he kept on driving and she got pissed and jumped his ass. I think he was scared, and I said,"Don't worry, tough guy. Don't be scared. The little girlie girl will protect you."

It was funny. After the show was over, I laughed. I was worried about them, but they couldn't find their ass with both hands.

But there was something about Autumn that I liked. She was different from the rest of the Bigfoot hunters, so I followed her progress on the show and checked out her website. After awhile, I decided that if I ever needed some Bigfoot help, she would be the one to contact. Little did I know that a few years later, I would do just that.

Our first contact was an email or two, followed by a two-hour phone call. She listened to what I had to say and didn't judge me or call me a liar. So I let my guard down too much and told her more than I had intended to. All I wanted was a little information; I wanted to know if other people were having the same thing going on that I did. She was easy to talk to and as she asked me questions, I tried not to say too much… but before I knew it, I had said too much.

After we ended the call, I was kicking myself, saying, "Why can't you keep your big mouth shut? Now she'll want to come down here and see the Big Guy and bring a whole herd of dumb-asses with her." I was afraid of what would happen or who she would tell. I wanted to keep my secret.

But after each call, I trusted her a little more and looked forward to our weekly talks. After a while, I began to think of her as a friend - and a better friend I have never had. She's the only person I would let come near my Big Guy because she understands their ways and I think I could trust her with it.

Because of who I am, I'm not quite there yet. Someday, I hope that will change and I'll ease up some and let her in. Trusting is a hard thing for me to do... and it's hard for the Big Guy, too.

–3–

PROOF & PICTURES

Mike first emailed me in September of 2009, after I'd published a video blog on YouTube about long-term witnesses and the need for researchers to treat habituations with care and respect. Our correspondence began tentatively.

I'm the single Mom of a toddler trying to support my daughter, care for her full time and run OregonBigfoot.com in my "free" time. Mike's email came in amongst hundreds of others that week that I barely had time to look at. The tone of his initial email was cautious, reserved - but as I skimmed it, it struck a chord in me. He said he had been interacting with a creature for several years and wanted to tell someone about it, but was concerned about harm coming to it.

I've received many similar emails over the years from individuals claiming to have ongoing interactions. I understand the desire to contact someone to validate their experience and the conflicting reticence to do so for fear of what might descend upon them, and the Bigfoot, if they contact the wrong person. I also remembered all the times I'd been contacted by folks who claimed ongoing encounters but whose stories, upon further investigation, appeared to be less-than-compelling. But, as always, I initially gave Mike the benefit of the doubt. I replied carefully in an attempt to let him know that I was aware of the delicacy of the situation. If this man *was* having ongoing encounters, I knew that he couldn't have chosen a more appropriate researcher with whom to share his experiences. I also knew that it would take a great deal of time and patience on my part to ensure *him* of that, as well as a great deal of time and patience on his part to assure *me* that he wasn't pulling my leg.

He replied a short time later with a few more details. I was intrigued.

First: you can't tell anyone about this. Anything I show you or tell you must stay between us. I have had many run-ins with these [Bigfoot researchers] online and I don't want anyone to know where this place is. I've seen what they do and they will chase them away and ruin it.

I've built a trust with this one and I would like to show someone, but what worries me is what will happen if I bring a stranger around. Will he run away and not come back? Will it make him not trust me? What do you think he would do? And how would you protect them from people once the word gets out? You know what will happen.

He's not tame but he'll come up to me because I bring him food. He loves fresh fruit like peaches and pears, and he can eat a lot.

I have been close enough to touch him. The smell is really bad but you get used to it after a while. I have to be careful when I'm around him and not turn my back on him. He lets me know that he can kill me whenever he wants. Sometimes it gets scary and I have to back away. I always carry a gun, just in case.

Sometimes when I bring him food, he will chase me away. I back away and watch from a distance.

I will tell you this: they seem to be driven by hunger. They are always looking for food and that, I think, is the key. Wood-knocking and making noise only lets them know that humans are in the area and they run away. And that's why I think they are hard to find - they hear people long before they see them.

I'm no expert but I have seen what they do when they hear a human. They hide, they run, they don't want to be seen.

If you can let me know what you'll do if I show you this place and them, it would be a big help to me. Whatever it is will have to be low key - do you know what I mean?

I have kept this secret for ten years and I don't mind going for another ten if I have to. The Big Guy comes first and what's best for him is what I will do… as soon as I know what is.

Thanks,

Mike

    I re-read Mike's email with one question in mind. Were his claims legitimate? While I've worked with many long-term witnesses over the years who have shared details of their limited interactions with Sasquatches, most of these tend to occur at a "safe" distance and consist of brief glimpses or distant sightings. This man's inference of regular face-to-face contact made me pause. Nothing in his email smacked of make-believe or boasting. In fact, he sounded very matter-of-fact and not as though he was sensationalizing the situation (which is often what a hoaxer will do). Nor was there any detail that didn't make sense to me, given everything I felt I'd come to understand about the nature of these creatures. Was it possible that he was experiencing exactly what he claimed? Or was he putting me on? And, if so, to what end?

I wrote back to him, ensuring him of the confidentiality of his identity and location, and did my best to answer his questions.

If you bring someone in, how the creature will react depends upon how that person behaves. If they are invasive, yes, you stand to lose your habituation. But I can't say more than that unless I fully understand the circumstances of what you're experiencing. I hope that makes sense.

Protecting them vs. 'proof' is something that I've mulled over for many years. I'm convinced that we don't know enough about them yet to really discern WHAT exposure would do to them... That's why the research is so important.

(My opinion on this, and many other things, would evolve drastically in the coming months.)

As our email exchanges continued, we began discussing this more in-depth. What would constitute proof and how would one go about proving Bigfoot exists in order to ensure their protection, without exposing them to harm in the process? Ironically, this subject was fresh in my mind; I'd recently been discussing this very topic with a witness who claimed to have substantial footage of these creatures and we'd been wracking our brains trying to muddle through the whole discovery/proof/protection scenario. We hadn't come to any conclusions - and here I was again, right back where I started.

Mike wrote:

I have photos and film and can prove that I am on the level but I won't send it over the net. I want to hang onto it for now. How can you tell people where they are and still protect them? That's the problem. Can you tell me what kind of proof I need to get that will stand up without a body? I can get whatever is needed but what will it take?

He mentioned a local professor who might be able to help him. I cringed. I had doubts that an academian would adequately understand or respect the delicacy of the situation and I had visions of statisticians and cold "proof-seekers" invading Mike's space.

But as I thought long and hard about Mike's questions before replying, I realized that I really didn't have an answer, either. What *would* happen if definitive evidence of Bigfoot's existence, the kind that would constitute "proof", were brought forth? What would that evidence entail?

I finally concluded that I didn't have enough information to say for sure… but I figured gathering the best evidence possible couldn't hurt while he had the opportunity to do so, as long as it was done carefully and respectfully. He could hold onto it while we considered what to do with it. If the situation were legitimate, I knew how rare this opportunity was and felt that it was worth a shot. I didn't know of anyone else who could readily obtain the kind of physical evidence necessary to avoid the perceived necessity of "a body".

I wrote him back:

Discovery and exposure of these guys is something that I've mulled over since I started doing this twenty years ago. Because Mom and I had a sighting when I was very young and had them roaming around in our back yard, I've always felt very protective of them. I know folks who are hell-bent on obtaining "proof" and presenting it to the world at ANY cost, but I've never felt like that. I think it may be important to classify them in order to protect them, but doing so should be thought out carefully. There are folks out there, especially in the South, who "sport hunt" these Guys. I can't tell you how WRONG I think that is, and legislation protecting them would hopefully inhibit that.

Now, specifically, to answer your first question, "How can you tell people where they are and still protect them?" You can't. That's the short answer. :) I would recommend that any witness who has built trust with one or more be VERY careful whom they invite into that space. That includes "professors". While academia generally ignores this subject, all it takes is for one person, professor or not, to come in and "take over" your habituation, do something wrong, and you've not only lost the habituation, you've put these guys in danger as well by exposing their whereabouts to some well-meaning science-type who doesn't understand the delicacy of the situation.

I am working with several people in hopes of protecting them. But simply providing proof isn't enough. If we prove THAT they are, that's one thing. But not being able to show WHAT they are... who ultimately has jurisdiction at that point? Are they animal or human? Are they protected under an endangered species act, or protected under a law that affords them the same rights as any other person?

A photograph that simply shows the creature will never constitute proof and won't accomplish what you're hoping for. The first thing is to prove, beyond a shadow of a doubt, that they exist. It's only half of the equation, but it's a start.

With that in mind, clear videographic documentation of obtaining physical evidence from the source and then providing that evidence with a chain of evidential custody would be ideal. For instance, sitting down with one and grooming him with a clean hairbrush ON VIDEO, then placing the hairbrush in a clean plastic bag ON VIDEO would be good. You could send me the hairbrush and I could immediately send it off to someone to have DNA testing done. Acting as a third-party buffer between you and the different parties working on the evidence ensures that no one institution knows too much about you or where you are... protecting your location and your Guy. Saliva might work as well... if you could get him to chew on something, or lick a piece of something with peanut butter on it... again on video, then carefully place that object in a plastic bag, on video, while wearing surgical gloves...

Fingernail clippings, hair (with root attached), saliva... all of these things contain DNA. Even a scab, some dandruff... if you could scratch his back, say, and have some hair and skin cells fall into a clean paper or plastic bag... these are all means of obtaining that evidence, but it would require close contact and preferably video proof of obtaining it.

Once the DNA results were in, the next step would be to build a complete scientific case study with other supporting evidence. This would include images (that's when they come in... they're not proof but they're important to support the evidence and determine what happens next), video, footprints, footprint casts, audio recordings and detailed observations. At that point, a scientific paper would be submitted to the scientific establishment for peer review - a name and classification, based upon the evidence, would be suggested in the paper. This is the important part, and where all of the other evidence and observation come into play... whether this thing is classified as an animal or a human. Because the type of legislation put in place to protect it and the agency that was contacted would depend upon it.

I would be more than happy to provide any help to you in this that I can, if this is what you want to do. Because I'm concerned about their welfare and don't want them exposed unless protection is assured, YOU can rest assured that anything I do will be done with that thought in mind first and foremost. I spend my life trying to educate people about these creatures and understand them myself, all the while walking a fine line not to disclose any information that would allow them to come to harm.

My thoughts on this were a work-in-progress, and I knew it. But I could only give him a glimpse into the same things I'd been taking into consideration and continue the dialogue from there.

Mike and I discussed his photographs over the phone a short time later. "Are they clear?" I asked.

"Well, they were taken with a disposable camera without a flash... but they're as clear as if I was taking a picture of your dog or something, if that's what you mean."

"How did you manage to get them developed?" I asked. I'd wondered about that before. If you had photos of a Bigfoot on film, how *would* you go about getting them developed?

"Wal-Mart," he said, surprising me. "You know, I thought about that after I took the pictures. Where could I take them to have them developed? I just took them to Wal-Mart. When the girl behind the counter handed me my pictures, she asked about them. I told her I was working on a movie, and that it was a movie prop. A guy in a suit. "That's a pretty good suit,' she said."

I chuckled.

In the past, witnesses have claimed to have photographs, only to produce blurred, shadowy images (affectionately referred to as "blobsquatches"), or they come up with some convenient justification or wild excuse why the photos ultimately did not materialize. I didn't get too excited about the idea that Mike had photos. At this point, I was still feeling him out to determine if what he was telling me was true or not. While I still didn't sense any red flags, I also wasn't born yesterday. So I continued to withhold judgment and see where this led.

Not long after our phone call, I received this strange email:

Hi Autumn,

I wanted to thank you once again for the help and to let you know that I no longer wish to pursue anything with the Bigfoot.

I am sorry for any inconvenience I may have caused you.

I enjoyed our talk and e-mails and had hoped we could become friends. But people have made it impossible for me to go forward with it at this time.

I should have never told anyone. It was a mistake on my part, thinking I could trust my friends. It is amazing to me what lengths some people will go to in order to get what they want.

I don't blame you for anything that happened - it was not your fault in any way. I think you were just the trigger that set it off. I found out that some of my things were taken from me and sold, and I had no idea until a few days ago. I found out who did it and got him to confess - and to say the least I have one less friend. They also screwed up my laptop really bad and it's still not working right. My geek said I will more than likely have to get a new one.

Oh, by the way, I will get some new photos for you so you won't think I'm nuts or something and you can do what you want with them. I owe you that much.

Thanks,

Mike

I immediately called Mike and listened, a little incredulously at first, to his story.

Apparently, his photographs of the creature were sitting in a manila envelope in a briefcase in a rented storage unit. After our call, he went to retrieve them – and found they were gone. They were the only thing that was missing. Since he was the only one with a key, he had a hard time fathoming how that could be.

I groaned inwardly and knew what my peers would say if they were in this situation. *How convenient… missing photographs… here we go…* But I stopped that train of thought immediately. I liked Mike a lot and I still wanted to give him the benefit of the doubt. Besides, *something* about his story so far had rung true to me. I couldn't yet put my finger on it. Once again, I decided to withhold judgment and hear what he had to say.

He said he'd racked his brain trying to figure out where they could have gone. "All day, I thought about it. And then I realized… there was only one other person who'd ever had access to that storage unit."

Mike had told me that he'd shown the photos to a friend at one point. He'd admitted to his friend that he'd seen the Skunk Ape from time to time while out in the swamp, but didn't give any specifics. His friend had taken a particular interest in their monetary potential. "You could sell those to the National Enquirer for $100,000, at least!" the friend said. Mike demurred. The photos weren't for sale.

Several weeks later, Mike's friend had asked to borrow money. Mike refused. "He still owed me the money that I loaned him before. I wasn't about to loan him no more."

Shortly after that, Mike asked his friend to help him move a couple of things at the storage unit. "The first thing he asks me when he sees the briefcase sitting there is, 'You still got those pictures of that Skunk Ape?' I told him, 'Yeah, and don't you touch that briefcase.' We moved the stuff, and then I went to the office to pay the storage bill. That must have been when he took 'em."

Mike called his friend, who had miraculously come up with the money he needed shortly after that. After multiple threats and guilt trips, the man came clean.

Apparently, his "friend" had stolen the photos that day while at the storage unit and shoved them up his shirt. He had then contacted someone through the internet and told him he had photographs. A man came to meet with Mike's friend, offering money for the photos. When pressed for information regarding where they came from, the friend offered that Mike knew where there was a Skunk Ape – had regular interactions with it, in fact. The man offered him additional money for more information about Mike.

"My friend said he got into the little book in the cab of my pickup where I keep all of my personal information, wrote all of it down, including my social security number, email address and passwords and sold them to the guy. So now this guy not only had all of my pictures of the Skunk Ape, he also had access to all of my email accounts. He must have been monitoring them, because as soon as I started writing to you about it, I got an email from this anonymous email address saying that I shouldn't be talking to you, that Autumn Williams is just in it for the money."

(At this point, I rolled my eyes. Yeah, I was in it for the money, all right. Researching Bigfoot was so "profitable", I was living with my kid in the middle of nowhere in a drafty cabin, eking out an existence as a work-at-home Mom so I could find the time to follow my passion.)

He said that he participated in a nasty email exchange with the anonymous e-mailer. "This guy had my pictures and now he wanted me to quit working with you and work with him instead. I told him there was no way he was ever going to find out where my Skunk Ape was, and if he showed his face anywhere around me or my swamp, I'd go Skunk Ape on his ass. I also told him that if I did get anything else, that I'd share it with you. Not him."

I asked Mike if he still had the negatives. "No. The whole lot of it - the photographs and negatives - was in that envelope."

Mike was clearly devastated. When he first discovered the photos were missing, he wasn't completely convinced that I didn't have something to do with it (which told me that Mike still didn't quite trust me). By the time he'd emailed me and we talked on the phone later that day, he had grilled his friend and realized I wasn't involved, but he was still disheartened and ready to throw in the towel. "Ever since I started talking to you about this, it just seems like everything's gone to shit. It ain't your fault," he added. "It just feels like I never should have opened my mouth."

I thought about the guy who had purchased the pictures. Obviously, he had to know that the pictures were sold illegally - that the photographer, and therefore the legal copyright holder, had not agreed to sell them. He had purchased stolen goods. And the personal information that Mike's friend sold him bordered on identity theft. The pictures could never be published, or Mike would have a case for a lawsuit and his friend could be subpoenaed to testify. So what was the point?

Was I surprised that someone would go to those lengths in order to attempt to gain control of that kind of evidence? Unfortunately, I wasn't. I'd been the victim of similarly shady practices and knew that some people's ethics left much to be desired; especially when pictures, video or other "proof" of Bigfoot's existence was concerned. To many, the phrases "Bigfoot pictures" and "big money" are unfortunately synonymous.

Mike said, "I'm pissed, because I was going to show you the pictures. I figured it was time for me to put up or shut up. Not only that, I've lost a friend over this deal and now someone knows more about me than I've told even you."

Ironically, I hadn't ever pressured Mike to see the photos. I figured that if he did have any, and at some point felt comfortable enough to share them with me, he would. In the meantime, I'd simply chosen to continue to work with him and see where this led. After all, what did I have to lose by trusting him, besides some time and energy?

−4−

TRUST

After the photograph fiasco, Mike began to open up a little more. Was it was my willingness to accept his explanation about the stolen photos? Or the fact that I was willing to listen to him regardless of whether he produced evidence or not? I didn't know. He still seemed to need to share his story with someone, and I was determined simply to be a sounding board for him.

I had come to enjoy his wit, the strange dichotomy of coarse language and intelligence, and his sometimes-wicked brand of humor that would catch me off guard and often cause me to burst into laughter. I realized that our relationship was moving from that of witness and researcher into the realm of genuine friendship. I liked Mike.

His personality was complex and multi-faceted. On one hand, he came off as a rather gruff, distrusting, no-nonsense guy who didn't put up for one second with anything that he considered "bullshit". He was prickly at times, quietly reserved at others. He thought things through before he said them, sometimes stopping in mid-sentence to digress and instead explain in detailed metaphor. It often felt like his trust was on the end of a short rope that he would yank back if he had the slightest indication that I was going to betray him, and I found myself treading delicately. But there was another side to Mike as well... a deeper part of him that I caught glimpses of through the cracks in his deliberately rough defenses. An inherent quality that he appeared determined to hide. A big grin split my face the moment I realized it.

Underneath it all, Mike was a big softie.

This became even more apparent when Mike began telling me about his experiences in detail.

When someone relates an encounter to me verbally, I usually ask him or her to fill out a sighting questionnaire. When the witness puts the story into written format, it ensures that all of the details and pertinent information is retained accurately for posterity. But I was beginning to get the impression that Mike's experiences were so far beyond most witness' solitary, incidental sightings, that the format of a sighting questionnaire would be useless. I hadn't even bothered to take notes in the beginning, since he didn't want me to share the information anyway – and at this point, I was so far behind, I felt that if I attempted to write down the things he'd told me, I'd never catch up.

During one of our now-regular Saturday phone calls, I asked him tentatively, "How would you feel about writing down your experiences?"

He expressed reluctance – more about the writing than the sharing. "I don't talk right," he said. "People are always making fun of the way I talk. I don't write no better."

"The way you speak has nothing to do with what you say," I told him, gently. Mike was exceptionally astute and his particular "dialect", as it were, had no bearing on that. To my Northwest-grown ears, his distinctive drawl was rather endearing. Nevertheless, I didn't press the issue.

Several days later, Mike sent me an email. He'd created a private document online that only he and I had access to, and sent me the link.

Like most witnesses, Mike hadn't begun to talk about his experiences until long after they had begun. However, unlike many long-term witnesses I'd worked with, Mike seemed very reluctant to *interpret* anything, which was one of the things that made him so credible from day one. I was used to dealing with witnesses who had struggled to make sense of their encounters and would inevitably end up interpreting their limited observations through whatever belief system or understanding of the world they held. By the time they related their story to me, they had usually woven elaborate explanations for what had occurred. At that point, it was up to me, as a researcher, to separate the wheat from the chaff, the facts from the interpretation.

Mike just told what he saw, what he smelled, what he heard; both on the phone – and now in this document.

As I started to read, I was floored. I had expected a few brief notes about his experiences. Instead, what I discovered when I opened the document was pages upon pages of single-spaced type: detailed interactions from day one, commentary on the creature's behavior and eating habits, and his occasional thoughts on why the creature might have behaved the way he did. He had touched on many of these events in our talks; but even then, I had no idea of the *extent* of Mike's interactions or his knowledge of the swamp and these creatures in it. It seemed that despite his persistent distrust for me because of my status as a "researcher", Mike was somewhat relieved to be unburdening himself of his secret.

I devoured the text in one sitting, my eyes glued to the screen. Suddenly, so many of the questions that had plagued me during a lifetime of wondering and analyzing were being addressed, one by one, in the small and stunning details of Mike's unique interactions with this creature.

I was happy to see that he had started at the very beginning.

(Mike's writings to me – those that he has given me permission to publish – are included in this book. I've edited them only for spelling and punctuation. I have intentionally left Mike's unique blend of grammar, syntax, and vernacular as it is. It is a part of who he is and I believe it's important for you to hear his "voice".)

It was the summer of 1998. I was walking on a sandbar far up a river in Florida where I live. I looked down and saw the biggest footprints I ever saw. They were at least sixteen inches long and seven inches wide and they were about three inches deep. I followed them along the riverbank until they disappeared into the woods.

This place is fifteen miles from the nearest town and you can only get there by boat. Off the main river, there is a small creek that winds deep into the swamp and the trees don't let in much sunlight, so it's dark even in the daytime. The swamp is thousands of acres surrounded by woods and planted pines. All total, there are millions of acres of wild land to roam, with few people. At the end of this creek, I have a camp – the only high ground in this part of the swamp.

The ground is covered with knee-high ferns and is soft and wet with a strong smell of rotting leaves. The canopy overhead is so thick that it makes you feel like you're inside a building. At night, it gets so dark that without a light you might as well be walking around with your eyes closed.

After I saw the footprints, I wanted to see what made them. I started to go back there as much as I could, hoping to get a look at what I knew was a Skunk Ape. I would spend all day and night walking and wading around the swamp looking for him. At night, I could hear him scream. It would make the hair stand up on the back of my neck. It was a lonely scream, almost a cry, and I would call back, my voice echoing through the swamp. It would be quiet for a while and then he would scream again. I would always call back to let him know he wasn't alone. I felt sad for him. It was the saddest thing I ever heard and I knew how he felt.

I didn't like people much and chose to spend most of my time alone. Even as a child, I never felt like I belonged, and was always on the outside looking in. That lonely cry in the night touched me deep inside. I wanted to reach out to him. I felt drawn to him – it was like he was calling to me.

As time went on, I would see fleeting glimpses of him; a shadow moving in the swamp, always keeping his distance. I would move toward him, trying to get a closer look but he would vanish as I got nearer. I needed to bring him to me, but how? What kind of bait would I use? What would make him want to come to me?

At first, I would leave fruit out in the swamp but he never found it. I thought he couldn't smell it, so I got some scented candles and would light them, thinking he would smell them and come to see what it was and find the fruit I had left for him. But it didn't work. I tried everything. If it smelled, I tried it.

Then, one day, I saw incense in a store and thought, 'These things smell!' So I bought a handful of cinnamon ones and headed back to the swamp.

I walked around, found out where he was, and moved around so I was upwind from him. I took the whole bunch, wrapped a rubber band around them, and lit them all at once, putting them on a stump. I put a bag of overripe peaches on the ground and moved ninety degrees to one side so he couldn't smell me. I walked about one hundred yards out, lay down behind a deadfall, and waited for him to come. In a little while, through my field glasses, I saw him coming... moving slowly through the trees, stopping to test the air and to look around. (They are very smart. They know when something is not right, and he wasn't taking any chances.)

He slowly walked up to the stump, picked up the incense, smelled it, and then put it to his mouth as if to taste it. I think it burned him because he threw it down and stepped back and looked around. It seemed like he knew I was around but wasn't sure where I was.

He bent down, picked up the bag of peaches, and started to eat, looking around to see where I was. After he got done eating, I stood up and yelled, 'My name is Mike and I want to be your friend.'

I had taken off my ghillie suit... I wanted him to see who was talking to him. He froze and stared at me and I turned and walked away, not looking back. I wanted him to know that I was not going to hurt him and that the next move was his to make.

Somehow, Mike had sensed something that seems imperative in gaining the trust of a Bigfoot: he understood that he needed to allow *him* to remain in control.

I had learned this same bit of crucial information many years ago from a long-term witness in Northern California.

This witness, whom I'll call Michelle, contacted me via email about her habituation. She had been recovering from an illness and was loaned a house by a musician friend of hers who was often on the road. She moved into the small domed-shaped home in the woods and wasn't aware that there was anything strange going on until she was lying out sunbathing in the nude one afternoon. There wasn't supposed to be anyone around, so when she heard a noise, turned, and saw a big, hairy *thing* staring at her, she was understandably shaken.

Her encounters around her home with what she also called the "Big Guys" continued for almost ten years before I met her. She and I spent nearly two years corresponding before we finally set a date to meet at her house. It took that long for us to fully develop friendship and trust, and by the time she finally invited me down, I felt justified in spending the time and money on the trip.

She had moved a few miles down the road from the friend's borrowed cabin, but still had access to the property. These are excerpts from my journal during that trip:

On May 26, 2000, my partner Bob and I arrived late – about 11 p.m. We set up the tent in the meadow in front of the new house and Bob lay down, tired from the long drive. Michelle and I sat on a stump there in the meadow, listening to the night sounds. We heard many strange sounds that night: a high-pitched whistling scream in the distance intermixed with dog or coyotes barking, a loud screech like an indrawn breath, a lower-pitched "looooooodle, looooooodle" sound that, eerily, was more said than sung, and several "roosters" crowing back and forth in the darkness between 2 and 3 o'clock in the morning, one of which <u>coughed</u> while crowing.

About an hour later, as I lay in the tent, something big ran by and threw an empty 55-gallon trashcan up against the side of the house.

The following night, Michelle asked if we'd like to go to the old place and go for a hike. Bob was nervous and reluctant because it was dark, about 11 p.m. – but he agreed. I was nervous, too, about going in the dark... especially when Michelle explained that we would be hiking deep into the woods and that the other researcher who was visiting refused to come. But I was excited, too. What an adventure!

The neighbors living in the dome house weren't home. They had four large dogs running loose that we had to contend with that barked and growled but stopped at the gate as we walked the road into the woods. They refused to follow us any further.

We followed Michelle about a half mile or more back into the canyon on a single-track trail, over logs and through blackberry bushes, over two small creeks, until we reached the big rock where she feeds her "Big Guys". After flicking about seven ticks off my pants, we settled down on top of the rock and she began to call them.

I was nervous and excited; I kept shaking involuntarily despite my best efforts to stay calm. We sat there for about half an hour and soon I began hearing what I can only describe as stealthy noises coming from two areas in front of us. It sounded as if SOMEONE were sneaking up on us. I could hear quiet and slow but distinct bipedal footsteps coming towards us from ahead and slightly to the right, and I began to hear something shuffling around to our left about twenty feet out.

For the next few minutes, we sat and listened, hearing shuffling sounds and things moving about quietly. I concentrated on just trying not to shake, and Michelle held my hand to calm me down. She also had me "pet" Bob's head, to "groom" him. She said seeing me do so would relax them. Once or twice, we heard whistles from down in the hollow or back up on the ridge. Finally, Michelle took the banana I'd brought (it was what I threw in my backpack), broke it into pieces, threw it out in front of the rock and said we should head back up the canyon.

"We're leaving?" I asked.

"We have to allow them to remain in control," she said.

She explained that they would come get the food if they wanted it and would follow us out. Bob muttered something to the effect of "Oh, great!" and I grinned. His nerves were shot. Mine weren't much better, but I wasn't ready to quit yet.

We hiked about halfway back down the trail until Michelle suddenly said, "Okay, this is good", and arranged the blanket in the middle of the path. We all sat down on it. She said it would take about ten minutes for them to come and, sure enough, about ten minutes later we heard those same crunching footsteps pass by on either side of us. It was a deeply vulnerable feeling to be sitting down in the dark in the presence of what sounded like several huge "somethings" tromping around. But I understood now that that was the point: to submit, to trust, and to give in to the experience.

We heard others coming. Every now and then there were whistles near the footsteps; quiet, discreet sounds, an almost "Hey!" kind of a whistle, of short duration, low-to-high pitched, and subtle – no louder than a bird. One of them passed us by completely and headed up the trail behind us. A minute or two later, it broke a branch that sounded about as big around as my femur... KEEEE-RACK!... and stomped around a bit. Michelle whispered, "I think it's doing that for Bob's benefit... letting him know who's boss." I don't think Bob was of a mind to argue.

At one point during all of this, I had to pee, and I simply couldn't hold it anymore. It happens when I get nervous. I walked a few short feet away from the blanket and squatted next to a tree in the pitch-blackness, all the while wondering if something was going to snatch me up and whisk me away with my pants around my ankles. I also worried about ticks and mosquitoes biting my behind. I'm a worrier, I guess. I managed to brave all the bugs and the Big Guys and sat down on the blanket, finally able to concentrate again... and that's when things got really interesting.

I don't know if my nature show had something to do with it, but once I sat back down, our forest visitors began to move around in earnest. I heard shuffling around us in all directions, and suddenly Bob said that he saw a figure walk by on the small ridge to our left. It blotted out part of the dimly lit sky for a moment. I turned to look as he whispered, "Look up there! Something just walked between those trees!" By the time I looked, it had moved on.

Moments later, I felt prickly... the hair stood up on my neck and I heard stepping, a settling, and a strange creaking sound very close to my left side, which faced the woods. It sounded the way my knee-joints creak sometimes when I crouch down. Then, suddenly, I smelled it –as if someone had opened a sewer line. There were three separate, DISTINCT whiffs, or puffs, of odor. It carried to my nose like cigarette smoke does – strong and eye watering. I whispered to Michelle, "I think one is right here behind the bush to my left." I reached my hand out as I asked,

"What happens if I reach out to it?" She whispered back, "Don't be surprised if he touches you." I jerked my hand back. I wasn't ready for that.

I wanted to do something to interact with this thing I couldn't see. I turned and smiled gently in the direction of the bush – and the fear shut off as if someone had flipped a switch. Suddenly, I simply wasn't afraid anymore. I heard rustling as whatever-it-was moved back up the hill. I sat there, filled with peace and awe and amazement, as the sounds around us continued.

The one on the trail ahead of us, ahead and to the left, whistled several times and the one directly to the right rustled the leaves and moved around a lot – then things became quieter. Bob was complaining that his stomach was hurting due to nerves, bad food, or both and we decided to leave.

As we hiked out, I could hear at least one of them walking parallel to us, whistling intermittently. It stopped at the bottom of the road near the incline that would take us to the house. Strangely, the dogs had stopped at the top – almost as if there were a barrier of several yards that neither would cross.

I think the thing that struck me the most was how quiet, stealthy, and discreet Michelle's Big Guys were.

When I see researchers running around wearing camouflage and talking about tracking them and trying to beat them at their own game on their turf, I just laugh.

Trust. It would become a central theme in my journey to understanding these creatures – as well as those who interact with them.

−5−

WINNING THE LOTTERY

By the time Mike and I came to know one another, I'd long since realized something else that I believe shaped my understanding of his particular situation: gathering "proof" and building rapport with these creatures, in many ways, appeared to be mutually exclusive.

Asking for physical evidence and photographs is among the first things most researchers naturally do when presented with a witness claiming ongoing encounters. "After all," they pointedly argue, quoting astronomer and popular science writer, Carl Sagan, "'*Extraordinary claims require extraordinary evidence*'."

As an inherently analytical thinker, I don't disagree with that statement. But what happens when the extraordinary circumstances tend to *preclude* the gathering of said evidence?

In the first place, it's common to assume that "ongoing encounters" means "frequent opportunities for Kodak moments". In most habituation cases I've investigated, it doesn't appear to be that simple. Many ongoing encounters are, for the most part, subtle interactions that occur at a distance. Actual sightings, as I've mentioned before, are generally brief; allowing the witness just enough of a glimpse of the mischief-maker to understand what they're dealing with, often to their shock and surprise.

I recently asked a researcher I know the following question: "If you had a chance to prove that these creatures exist, or to create an ongoing interaction with them that would afford you the opportunity to learn more about them... and those two options were *mutually exclusive*... which would you choose?"

"I'd prove it."

He answered without hesitation – and completely missed the point.

His answer illustrated perfectly why more researchers don't pay attention to long-term witness encounters. The idea of simply *experiencing* something, without feeling the need to prove it to the world, does not fit into their paradigm. The idea that trying to gather proof may *prevent* the very circumstances in which proof could be obtained is, apparently, an even harder concept to grasp.

Researchers rarely have sightings. Witnesses have sightings. And the reason for this, I firmly believe, is that witnesses don't run around behaving like researchers. The very actions of researchers in the forest are counter-productive to close interaction. So how can you hope to "prove" the existence of something when your behavior interferes with building the trust necessary to get close enough to acquire proof?

Or, as Mike says, "How can you reach out one hand in friendship – while holding a camera in the other?"

I noted from the outset that Mike's case was unusual: his was one of the few I'd encountered in which the witness was presented with ample opportunities to photograph the creature. And he had, apparently, in the past. But again, as we'll see later in this story, it turned out that it was not quite that simple. In fact, Mike very nearly paid the ultimate price for attempting to do so again.

Most importantly, most researchers fail to realize the emotional quotient involved in long-term witnesses scenarios. These witnesses inevitably describe to me a feeling of "bonding" with the creatures they interact with, and a reluctance to compromise the integrity of that bond. The closer the contact is, the closer the bond… and the more reluctant the witness is to provide a souvenir from Bigfootland, especially to those who make it clear that they don't understand or respect that bond in the first place. Enter the stalemate, the impasse that witnesses and researchers find themselves facing - and the reason most witnesses throw up their hands in disgust and walk away, going back to the woods and to interactions with these creatures that researchers can only dream of.

    Over the last decade, I've watched many long-term witnesses come forward on various public internet forums, attempting to share information about their encounters. And I've watched the research community, time and time again, wreak havoc on witness' peace of mind and self-esteem, ridicule them, question their credibility in ways that are sometimes downright cruel... all this, from a community who laments the fact that witnesses are not more eager to come forward and share their experiences.

    Researchers on these message boards routinely clamor for pictures. But as any good researcher will tell you, photographs will never constitute "proof". Those same photographs, were they offered, would immediately be held suspect. Particularly if they were clear. With the advent of digital photo manipulation, no image is believable anymore. Add to that the pervasive aura of distrust in the research community and any witness bringing forth pictures is merely setting themselves up for further attack.

Let's examine, for a moment, the concept of "proof". It's a complex subject, but in the end, perhaps *context* is what it all boils down to.

The first question that comes to mind is this: To prove, given the chance, or not to prove?

Please note how that question is worded. The topic that usually sets Bigfoot forums buzzing and starts heated disagreements and flame wars is "To kill or not to kill?" Most researchers generally fall firmly on one side of the fence or the other. But this topic, in my mind, encompasses far more than that.

What, ultimately, would constitute proof? What would a "proof" scenario look like? What are the possible ramifications, on our world and that of the Bigfoot, of proving that they exist? And, ethically, do we have the right to potentially destroy something simply to assuage our curiosity about it?

Many people believe that, in order to put the question of Bigfoot's existence to bed once and for all, only a body will do. A body on a slab, they argue, will tell us that they exist. It will prove *that* they are. But will it ultimately tell us *what* they are? And if a body is acquired, is the general public likely to ever hear about it? The consequences of disclosure will inevitably be taken into account by any agency or individuals involved in the dissemination of that information. Whoever has a body, or any kind of proof in hand, has the opportunity to make a bigger impact on this world than they may realize.

For the record, I have always been firmly against harming a Sasquatch in any way. (Except, perhaps, in self-defense – which would be a questionable scenario to begin with, since these creatures rarely seem directly aggressive unless stupidly provoked and whether killing something because you stupidly provoke it can really be considered "self defense" is another thing entirely.)

I don't believe we have the right to "take a specimen". Personally, it's a moral dilemma. Researchers talk about taking "just one" to put the subject to rest. Often, somewhere within all of the initial blood lust, there are vaguely altruistic murmurings about "proving they exist so they can be protected". This strikes me as being very shortsighted. First, I'm positive that one wouldn't be enough. Secondly, the idea that proving something exists will automatically cause us to subsequently protect it, with our track record of destroying most everything we touch, is just… well, rather asinine and smacks of arrogance and short-sighted ignorance.

"What is it?"

"I don't know! Let's kill it and find out! Wait… that sounded bad. I know: Let's say we're killing it so we can identify it and protect it!"

"But," those who are pro-kill say, "how can you prove it exists without a body? And how can you protect it if you can't prove it?"

First: are there ways to prove it exists – at least enough to garner protection – without a corpse or a captured creature? Second: who says we CAN protect them? Third: do they even NEED our protection? Finally: What would constitute "protection"?

Let's carefully examine what might happen to someone who *is* successful in obtaining a body.

It's a popular assumption that a dead Bigfoot would bring millions of dollars. And fame. Sounds great, doesn't it? So what's the downside?

Consider this scenario (which is entirely fictional, of course, but is certainly realistic):

Josh is an avid hunter. He lives in the south – land of the booger monsters. He's determined to bag himself a Bigfoot, become stinking rich and go down in infamy as the guy who proved it once and for all. Hell, maybe they'll even name it after him with one of those big, long scientific-sounding names, like *Joshipithecus Americanus*.

Josh and his buddy Carl head into the swamp for the day. They're accomplished trackers and have been following this booger for weeks. They're armed to the teeth, they aren't afraid of anything, and that sucker ain't gettin' away this time.

They hike two miles to the spot and climb into the deer stands just before dawn, high in the trees. They got here without speaking a word. They're scent-blocked, covered in camouflage and don't make a sound. Hand signals are all they need. They're good at what they do.

After an hour or so, Josh hears something moving through the swamp, coming at a good clip on Carl's right. He signals to Carl that he'll have a shot. In the gray morning light, he makes out a huge, hairy form moving through the cypress knees, almost gliding, making little sound as it moves through ankle-deep water. He waits. He knows he only gets one shot. He holds his breath as he pulls the trigger.

The shot hits its mark. Blood sprays from the creature's chest; it's a kill shot, just like he knew it would be. Some of those assholes on the forum said the gun wouldn't be big enough, but he knew better. He lets out an exhilarated whoop as the giant body falls backward into the water with a huge splash.

"You got him! You got the sonofabitch!" Carl yells.

The morning is preternaturally still as they climb down from the tree stands, adrenaline pumping. They slowly approach the huge, hairy body lying motionless at the edge of the bayou, guns trained on it. Josh approaches cautiously and kicks one enormous foot. It's heavy. Dead weight. Blood fills the dark, tea-colored water around the body. Its dark eyes are closed, the lips slack.

They just won the lottery.

Carl's voice breaks the silence. "Um… now what, dude?"

The thing is massive. Maybe 800 lbs.

"Now we drag his ass out of here and call the press."

Do Josh and Carl successfully drag the body out of the swamp? Or do they end up on a missing persons list because they didn't see the other two creatures watching from the trees back there in the bayou, who charge in screaming with bared teeth – another 1600 pounds of righteous fury – as the men try to put together the travois?

Perhaps they do manage to drag 800 pounds two miles back to the truck and somehow load the body in with Josh's winch. They get the body home, buy a freezer, and stuff the body in. Again, the question is raised. Now what?

They're in a hurry to make some money. Josh and Carl call the press. They tell CNN that they have a Bigfoot body on ice – a REAL one, "…not like them idiots from Georgia with a costume in a freezer" – and that CNN can have an exclusive on it for a million bucks. Then they call FOX News. They up the ante to two million and play the two networks against each other until they get an offer of $3.5 million. That calls for a high-five.

The film crew shows up. Our boys, proud as peacocks, tell how they tracked this thing and took it down successfully. CNN airs a full-hour special, the guys get paid, split the money and everything's great.

Suddenly, Josh and Carl are rich. And famous. Every media outlet in the country wants to interview them. They're a sensation, flying all over the country for interviews. Good Morning America. Letterman. The Discovery Channel contacts them about doing a special; they want to bring in scientists to examine the corpse. The local university wants a look. Every individual Bigfoot researcher in the free world is calling their home phone numbers, which were sniffed out and posted on a public forum fifteen minutes after the first CNN special aired. Within days, they're overwhelmed and decide to hire someone to deal with the media frenzy.

That gets expensive in a hurry... but heck, they're millionaires, and are being offered exorbitant amounts of money for appearance fees. One guy even offered to buy the thing for $10 million. Life is good.

Until the Feds get involved. Or the Department of Fish and Wildlife. Or The Department of Natural Resources. Or PETA. Maybe even the ACLU. The hammer of justice falls swiftly, and no matter whose jurisdiction it ultimately turns out to be, Josh and Carl will have bitten off far more than they can chew.

The men are arrested. Charges are brought against Josh and Carl for hunting an animal out of season without a license. Pending scientific study, murder or manslaughter charges may be brought as well. The body is confiscated by the courts as evidence and as multiple government and academic parties fight over who has jurisdiction of the corpse, Josh and Carl find themselves posting bail and hiring lawyers. Self-defense is out of the question since they've already crowed to the world how they were out to kill the thing and made no bones about how their skills and stealth got the job done. The lawyers tell them not to talk about the case anymore. So much for appearance fees.

Suddenly, there isn't enough money in the world to get them out of this mess.

By the time all is said and done, Josh and Carl will wish they had never, ever heard of Bigfoot.

While a body would allow for scientific examination and classification, and would therefore constitute "proof" of Bigfoot's existence to one and all, there is another important question that receives far less scrutiny.

Just because it *could* be proven... *should* it be?

People who believe that Bigfoot exists generally do so for a personal reasons. Maybe they've had a sighting, and that was proof enough for them. Or perhaps they've examined the masses of anecdotal evidence in the form of eyewitness encounters and have concluded that there is sufficient corroborating evidence to support its existence.

Likewise, skeptics are often skeptical for a reason. The idea of Bigfoot's existence threatens their "sensibilities", their dogma – be it scientific, religious, or otherwise.

A hunter who has spent thirty years hunting the same woods and has "never seen anything like that" might feel that the existence of such a creature threatens his perceived knowledge of everything that's in the woods. And maybe the thought of running into one just plain scares the daylights out of him deep down inside, so he discounts it because he's a big, burly fella and skeptical anger is more comfortable to him than fear. (He's woods-savvy, and knows what to expect when he's out there. Something in the woods that he doesn't understand scares him and takes away his feeling of control.)

A scientist who is snidely skeptical, explaining that "there simply aren't enough food sources available in the

Pacific Northwest" in an attempt to close the book on the subject, might feel deeply threatened by the idea that there are still things in this world that his many years of expensive and time-consuming education didn't cover. Accepting the idea that something like that exists, publicly, would threaten his credibility... and therefore his ego. (It's something he can't control with hard facts and data and place neatly in a little box marked "Explained".)

A deeply religious man might discount the existence of Bigfoot simply because it doesn't fit in with his belief system. (It threatens his carefully accepted dogma about how the world is and it scares him that there may be an unknown quantity out there that isn't explained within the context of his belief system.)

In all three of these examples, the *unexplained* causes the fear, and thus the carefully crafted yet vehement disregard for the creatures' existence. Something that is unexplained – and therefore not understood – cannot be controlled. Fear begets anger. That anger might be expressed in many different ways:

"What a buncha crap! I been in these woods 30 years and there ain't nothin' like that out there!"

"There aren't enough food sources to support an 800 lb. primate in the forests of North America, therefore they simply cannot exist."

"It doesn't say anything about Bigfoot in the Bible..."

The words are different. The 'logic" is different. The individuals speaking come from vastly diverse backgrounds. But the fear is the same.

People who vehemently dismiss the existence of Bigfoot do so because they feel threatened by the subject for one reason or another. Would they, then, put aside their fear and accept "proof"?

Some don't believe in Bigfoot because they're simply ignorant. It's not that they have a problem with its existence. They just don't know much about the subject at all, and don't care to. They disregarded Bigfoot's existence a long time ago based on what little exposure they've had to the subject: mainly tongue-in-cheek newscasters, misinformation in the press and a general apathy toward anything but the smarmiest and most sensational Bigfoot headlines in the mass media. "I thought that whole thing was proven to be a hoax years ago. Didn't some guy come forward and confess to making all those footprints?"

The root of the word "ignorance" is to *ignore*. It doesn't mean there isn't more information available. It just means these people aren't paying very close attention.

They are, very simply, not qualified to be skeptics. Skepticism has no weight, no credibility, when one's opinion is based upon bias, ignorance, disinformation or a lack of education.

So... what exactly would constitute "proof" for all of these skeptical folks?

Imagine the following scenario; one that Bigfoot researchers regularly dream of. A body is discovered. Scientists examine the body, determine it to be a North American bipedal primate of unknown origin. It hits the news. All of those skeptics are going to eat their words, right?

The hunter watches with mild interest. "Huh. Well, there ain't none of them things in *my* woods. I woulda seen him." He changes the channel.

The scientist now accepts the existence of Sasquatch because it's fashionable to do so. "We've determined that these creatures are omnivores and spend a great deal of their time searching for food." He never mentions the fact that he summarily dismissed their existence based upon a lack of viable food sources, and hopes no one brings it up. He's the guy everyone calls when they want an interview or a sound bite regarding Bigfoot… much to the chagrin of the layperson "researchers" who consider themselves experts on the subject.

The religious man carefully places the creature in amongst all of God's other "animals" and ignores any subsequent reports about their DNA being closer to ours than chimps...

The Ignorants? They remain ignorant. "I thought they killed that Bigfoot creature and dissected him." Because in their minds, there was always *only one* Bigfoot and the subject is no more important to them now than it ever was.

Will the body on a slab *really* "show all of the skeptics" and put an end to the mystery? In the end, who is the "proof" *for*? What purpose will it ultimately serve? Will it genuinely provide protection?

Growing up in Oregon, I saw firsthand the devastation on timber communities caused by the protection of the spotted owl. Imagine the impact a large, humanlike primate would create. Where would the funds for complex study and management of this new "wildlife" come from? Alternatively, if it's decided that they're something closer to human, would we attempt to round up the Sasquatch and stick them on "reserved" lands? How could we hope to contain something that wanders for a living and could snap us in half like a twig if we tried to contain it? Would we end up shutting down all the forestland to logging and recreation in order to protect this newly discovered species? Or send emissaries in to attempt to "civilize" them?

I suspect that, if government officials are aware of the existence of these creatures, the last thing they'd want is for the public to be aware of it. Public outcry would force the hand of the authorities to manage and protect something that is, inherently, unmanageable. Better to let it remain a myth.

–6–

TWO-DIMENSIONAL SASQUATCH

In 1967, Roger Patterson, with the help of Bob Gimlin, set out to film a Bigfoot documentary near Bluff Creek, CA. On October 20, Roger filmed 24 feet of color footage of a Sasquatch on a handheld 16mm Kodak movie camera. The footage has held up under decades' worth of scrutiny. While not "proof" of Bigfoot's existence, those images are the clearest and most compelling captured to date.

Nearly everyone in the free world has seen the footage of the creature they filmed that day, striding up Bluff Creek. It has been played and replayed *ad nauseum* as a curiosity and the images therein, especially frame number 352, have become synonymous with the subject of Bigfoot.

The only person still living today who actually *saw* this living, breathing individual, not on a flickering film screen but with his own eyes, is Bob Gimlin. Yet the Patterson/Gimlin Sasquatch, also known as "Patty", has become the poster child for nearly every print and news media dissertation on Bigfoot, serious or otherwise. The constant exposure has turned Patty, as the iconic depiction of "Bigfoot", into something of a celebrity.

This didn't dawn on me until after Mysterious Encounters began airing, and I started to experience the awkwardness of the "celebrity swoon".

Now, you probably only knew who "Autumn Williams" was if you were a Bigfoot aficionado, or liked watching professional bull-riding on OLN and your usual prime-time PBR schedule was rudely interrupted with "some show about Bigfoot", or were channel surfing and happened to land on it. Otherwise, you wouldn't know her from Adam. Or Eve, rather.

But those who found the show and tuned in regularly saw thirteen episodes of this blond girl running around the country chasing Bigfoot. Everyone became intimately acquainted with the inside of her nose thanks to that stupid "backpack" cam. Autumn and her deviated septum were blazoned across millions of TV sets in living rooms from Florida to Washington.

And something weird started to happen.

I first noticed it on the public Bigfoot forums. People began talking about me as if I were some*thing*… not some*one*. The initial criticisms of the show from armchair quarterbacks were brutal. "Autumn Williams" was fair game, and it was hunting season. I read lewd comments about my physical… erm… "attributes", snide commentary on everything from my clothing to my nose to my manner of speaking… Anything in the show that they didn't like was my fault. I was the host of the show, after all – therefore, I *must* have had complete control over every aspect of the series. I was publicly tried and found guilty of being less-than-perfect in a hundred different ways. And how dare I be? I was on their televisions, after all, and only perfect people end up on television!

It was hurtful. I had been a member of these forums and these peoples' peer in the research community for years and suddenly they were talking about me as if I didn't exist and couldn't read the horrible things they were saying. And I suppose, in a way, I *didn't* exist anymore. I had suddenly become two-dimensional. I was "different". I was on TV. I was suddenly, as one guy put it, "Ms. Hollywood".

After the initial hubbub died down, another equally disturbing aspect of the phenomenon began to take hold. People started acting… strangely. They'd hang back quietly at conferences, staring at me, finally coming up with a weird perma-grin and saying things like, "I've seen all of your shows. I can't believe I'm meeting 'Autumn Williams'. Will you sign this?" Or I'd call someone to discuss an issue they were having with logging in to their member's account on the website and they'd say, "I can't believe I'm talking to 'Autumn Williams'!" No one referred to me by my first name anymore, or a pronoun like, "you".

I went from being publicly tarred and feathered to dealing with star-struck "fans", all in the course of a few months. And I was completely bewildered. I was the same person I always was.

Somehow, I had suddenly become a two-dimensional thing on a screen. A poster child for a cause.

It dawned on me then. I kind of felt like Patty, the Patterson/Gimlin Sasquatch. An "icon", of sorts. And I didn't like it one bit.

We are constantly exposed to celebrities in two-dimensional settings. On TV. On film. In papers, magazines and print. We "learn" about them through those two-dimensional means. We think we know them. Their names become synonymous with what we think we know about them. The name "Michael Jackson" brings to mind all sorts of preconceived notions and connotations – some positive, many negative, but all are a conglomeration of what we've "learned" about that person through two-dimensional exposure. Did any of us really *know* him? Did we ever think about the fact that he might have woken up on a Sunday morning, maybe rubbed the goop out of his eyes, poured a bowl of cereal and channel-surfed, just like anyone else? Do we ever get past the sensationalism and picture celebrities that as real people?

If I've learned anything about "celebrity", it's that it is uncomfortable and often dehumanizing.

You can tell when you've become a celebrity, because people seem *surprised* to interact with you directly, living and breathing, in a three-dimensional real-world setting. And they let you know they're surprised: "I can't believe I'm actually talking to [insert full name here in lieu of the appropriate pronoun]!"

It would almost be funny… if it weren't so damned creepy.

That's why the paparazzi make the big bucks. It's unfathomable that a celebrity might actually drive through Taco Bell like everyone else… unless it's Britney Spears. (See how we think we understand people?) Capturing images of two-dimensional, icons doing everyday things in the "real" world is big business.

Hasn't "Bigfoot" become a celebrity of sorts? Isn't Patty's image instantly recognizable? And what are we, really, besides a bunch of Bigfoot paparazzi, running around with cameras trying to capture the "money shot" of this two-dimensional icon doing normal, everyday things in the "real" world?

"What's a picture like that worth?"

What was Patty doing on that fateful morning? What did she have for breakfast? Where was she going when she was captured on film, striding purposefully across that sandbar? What was she feeling? Where did she sleep later on? What was she thinking about these two little hairless fellas who pointed those things at her and showed such interest in her footprints?

How would *you* feel if someone walked up to you and said, "I can't believe you're real!"?

When we view Bigfoot superficially, as a two-dimensional subject, when we fail to read between the lines and understand the nature of that which we seek... we fail to find it.

This is never more apparent than when I take novice researchers into the field. They simply can't seem to wrap their brains around the *size* of a Sasquatch. We stand there in the dark and a stick snaps. Their flashlight clicks on immediately, pointed at the brush in front of them. I'll explain to them about the evils of shining flashlights at a Bigfoot later… for now, I take hold of their arm gently and still the frantic side to side scanning. "That's his crotch," I say with a grin, and lift their arm. "That would be his face."

But failing to fathom Bigfoot doesn't stop at size. More importantly, it's common misconceptions about the nature and behavior of the creatures that consistently cause researchers, also known as would-be witnesses, to miss the mark.

I've spent many years disagreeing with colleagues who are certain that Bigfoot is simply an animal - an "ape". The details and experiences Mike related to me have confirmed my suspicion that this species is very different from what most people *believe* it is. Bigfoot researchers interpret sighting reports with biases firmly in place, and they consistently miss subtle, telling details that would indicate that these creatures are far more intelligent and intuitive than they're given credit for.

Why else would Bigfoot research have been such an abject failure over the past several decades? Because erroneous preconceived notions won't get you very far when you're trying to "prove" the existence of something that you haven't even begun to understand. Especially if you're underestimating it.

The greatest irony? The majority of Bigfoot researchers are trying to prove the existence of a creature *that exists only in their minds.*

-7-

MEETING THE LOCALS

After Mike discovered the footprints on the sandbar, he was curious about the creature and began trying to track it. In doing so, he spent several years having little success. At first, he would spend weekends there; then, all of his free time in-between jobs. Eventually, Mike began spending weeks at a time in the swamp - living, as he puts it, "like a Skunk Ape".

It got to the point where I was going to find him if it killed me. I wasn't going to let some hairy-ass Skunk Ape get the best of me. So I kept going, but I needed a new plan. I needed to change the way I was thinking.

I was having some deep personal issues going on, so I withdrew into the swamp to get away from people and to find some solitude. This was my way of coping with the world. And in doing so, I was drawn into his. At times, I think I was becoming less human and more Skunk Ape. When I would see hunters in the swamp, I would hide from them, watching their every move. I would become a shadow moving from tree to tree, a stealthy creature of the swamp.

For about four years, I tried to get close to him. I would sneak around in a ghillie suit like a sniper. I would lie in the mud for hours, waiting for him to come close, but he always seemed to know I was there. I would climb trees, sit, and wait. I would sit in the creek with only my head above water, waiting for the bait to attract him. And sometimes when I would see him I would run toward him thinking I could catch up with him, but his walking speed is my running speed, so you can guess what his running speed is.

I would see him from a distance but I could never get close to him.

The day Mike put out the incense appears to have been a turning point. Until then, he'd been skulking around in the swamp trying to sneak up on the creature, even chasing it at times. On that particular day, stealth worked. But it seems that it was what Mike did afterward - standing up, greeting the creature, then deliberately walking away - that seemed to have the greatest impact.

That night, I was sitting by the fire, wondering if he would leave the area or stay around. Did I mess up and scare him off? I looked up, and at the edge of the firelight, there he was... standing there looking at me. He was big. I mean, really big. He stood there, not moving. His eyes glowed red in the light. I moved my hand down, resting it on my pistol, just in case.

After a while, I said, "You going to come in or stand there like a stump?" He huffed at me, turned around, and walked into the darkness.

I could hear him moving around behind me. I could smell him now. He was upwind and it was bad - like a wet, musky garbage dump. I waited to see if he would come closer, my back still to him and my hand still on my pistol. I waited.

It seemed like hours, but I slowly turned around and he was standing no more than twenty feet away. I stood up and said, "I'm Mike. This is my camp. Please come in and sit." He didn't move. "You wanna eat?"

I reached down, got a bag of apples, and tossed them to him. They landed at his feet. He took the apples, huffed at me, and walked into the night.

I was shaking... not scared, but excited.

Mike's approach – cautious, primarily *passive*, yet matter-of-fact and gently interactive - appeared to have the desired effect. The creature returned later that night, after midnight.

I sleep in a hammock I made from rope. I don't like to sleep on the ground and I won't sleep in a tent unless it's raining.

I was lying there, sleeping on my back with my arms across my chest, when I felt something bump my hammock, making it rock. I've had black bears come into camp and bump into me... so when I opened my eyes expecting to see a bear, imagine my surprise when I saw the Skunk Ape standing over me.

He had me... I had nowhere to run. I just lay there, not moving. He reached out and picked up my hand ever so gently and turned it over, looking at it, lifting my arm up and with the other hand stroking it, feeling it. He wasn't rough with me. It was like you would pick up a child's hand, making sure not to hurt it. I lay there with my eyes wide open, wondering what he would do next.

He looked, saw that my eyes were open, then put my hand down and walked away.

The next morning, I was getting ready to go fishing and was putting my cooler back in the boat. I turned around and there he was, standing about eight feet away. Scared the hell out of me!

I jumped back, falling backward into the boat and said, "Damn it, Snapperhead, you scared the crap out of me!" He stood there with this blank look on his face.

Getting to my feet, I looked over at my pistol hanging on the tree. He was between it and me. I was still not sure how safe I was around him and liked to keep it close just in case.

I stood there looking at him. I could not get over how big he was - all muscle and hair. His eyes were dark brown, his hair was black with a red tint when the sunlight hit it, and when he looked at me it was like he knew what I was thinking. It was like he was looking inside of me - like he understood what I was and that I was not a threat.

He backed up and looked around at the food I had out and looked back at me as if to say, "What you got to eat?" I slowly walked over to the table, put some fruit in a box, and held it out to him but he wouldn't take it. I put it down and backed up to give him some room. He picked it up and made some clicking sounds, and then growled and walked off.

It shook me up a little. I hadn't heard him come up and my back was only turned for a second. (He can be sneaky when he wants to.)

After I calmed down, I got in the boat and went downriver, fishing. I was gone most of the day.

I went back to camp to pack up and head home. I looked around to see if I could find him but he was nowhere in sight, so I took the rest of my food and left it for him.

As I turned out of the creek into the river, I saw him standing at the edge of the woods, watching me go. I stopped and stood up. Taking my hand and patting my chest over my heart, I held out my hand and said, "Goodbye, my friend. I'll see you soon."

I think he shook his head, like he understood. I'm not sure, but I left that day a different man.

It was the start of a friendship like has never been before and maybe never will be again. It made me look deep inside myself and find the part of me that I'd lost.

When Mike had begun to share his story with me over the phone, I was fascinated. He impressed upon me early on that he had not shared his experiences in detail with anyone... not even his siblings, or friends. There was only one friend who'd seen the photos – the one who'd stolen them. He'd never discussed his experiences with another researcher. His disdain for them was obvious; he'd lurked some on the internet, visiting websites and reading about Bigfoot researchers' work and was unimpressed. "I'm no expert," he'd remind me time and again, "but these guys don't know shit and they have no idea what they're dealing with. They just keep doing the same crap over and over again, then pat each other on the back and call themselves experts. The only thing they are expert at is doing it wrong. I have no use for any of them tree knockers."

If Mike had experienced all of these things, it seemed to me that he likely knew more about Bigfoot than anyone I'd ever met. IF. It was a big word. As a researcher, I had learned to reserve judgment - to allow the jury to remain out and keep both blanket skepticism and unconditional belief at bay as I gathered as much information as possible.

As I arrived at the sandbar early Saturday morning, I nosed my boat up on the sand to take a look around. I wanted to see if there were any tracks in the soft sand - and sure enough, there were, right along the edge of the water where anybody could see. I took my foot and rubbed them out. I didn't want anybody to see them. If people knew he was here, they might try to kill him as it seems everyone wants to see one dead. That's the only way they will believe that they exist - kill one and put him on display.

I got back in the boat and eased up the creek to my camp. It felt good to be back "home" after a long week of traffic and people.

I had stopped at the roadside fruit stand and bought one case of peaches, four bags of apples, six cantaloupes, one stalk of bananas... then thought I'd better stop by the store and get some more stuff. He looked like he could eat a lot. I wasn't sure what he liked to eat so I loaded up on food.

Pulling up to camp, I could see that all the food that I had left the week before was gone. I was hoping he was close by and I wouldn't have to wait too long to see him. I walked up and looked out into the swamp. No sign of him... but it was early and I had two days to find him so it was just a waiting game.

I loaded my pack with as much food as I could and headed off into the swamp. I had walked for about an hour and saw something moving behind me. It was him. He was tracking me.

I didn't find him. He found me.

(And that's the way it was. He had to come to me. If I walked toward him, he would disappear like a shadow, only to pop up somewhere else.)

He trailed me for a while and I lost sight of him, so I stopped and sat down on a log and waited. After a short while, I heard something behind me and turned around and he was there, not more than thirty feet away. Standing up, I patted my chest and held out my hand and said, "Hello, my friend. I'm glad to see you. Do you wanna eat?"

(I pat my chest and hold out my hand because I wanted to have a greeting and a goodbye for him - a way to talk, a starting or stopping point. He does this now when he sees me, too. It took a long time but he got it and we have our own little way of talking. At work, we use hand signals to talk that way. We don't have to get off our machines or yell over the noise… so I use them to talk to him. It works well and he learns fast. It is amazing how smart he is. I don't mean smart like a dog - I mean people-smart. He knows what's going on around him and understands what you want from him. But make no mistake about it: he is the boss of the swamp and you do things his way or not at all - a point he has driven home a time or two.)

I opened up my pack and put the food on the ground: some apples and peaches and a Blue Bird honey bun (which I would come to discover was his favorite), and stepped back.

He huffed at me to let me know that I was too close, so I moved back about fifty feet and sat down on the ground.

He squatted down and started to eat, watching me the whole time. I got up, patted my chest and waved my hand and said, "I've gotta go now. You know where to find me." I turned and walked away, not looking back. I wanted him to know that I was his friend and wasn't wanting anything from him.

Mike's repetitive behavior and his willingness to bow out of an encounter first communicated a lack of agenda on his part.

This guy was smart.

I didn't see him again until that night. He came up to the edge of camp but wouldn't come in. I don't think he liked the fire; it was a little big and hadn't burned down yet. I picked up some more fruit and a loaf of bread and took it out and set it on the ground, then went and sat down. He moved in, took the food, and walked away.

The next day, I got up and went down to the sand bar to see if he had been out there making tracks. I was glad to see that he hadn't. I wished to myself that he would stay off of there. But there wasn't much I could do - it was just a matter of time before someone saw his tracks and went after him.

(This used to worry me but I came to realize that he could take care of himself. Finding tracks and finding him were two different things...)

When I got back to camp, he was waiting for me. He was sitting on the ground, leaning back on his hands. When he saw me, he jumped up and moved back into the swamp at the edge of camp. I said, "Don't run off... stay and visit a while." After getting a soda from the cooler, I sat down and looked around at the camp. It was just like I'd left it - not a thing out of place. If he had been a bear, there would've been a big mess to clean up and no food left. But he didn't touch a thing. Did he respect my territory or was he just not hungry?

I looked at him standing there and said, "Thank you for not trashing my camp. You're a good man."

It was getting close to noon and I was hungry so I decided to cook me some eggs and Spam. I sliced the Spam up into cubes and put them in the cast iron pan. Food tastes better cooked in cast iron. I let the Spam fry for a while, and then poured the eggs over them. (I call it "Mike's Wilderness Mess.") I added some onion and green pepper and chopped potatoes, mixing it as it cooked. The whole time he was watching me cook, I could see his nose twitching back and forth. He knew he was smelling something good.

I said, "You wanna try some of this mess? It'll put a spring in your step and a smile on your face." He grunted and moved a bit closer. I think he was trying to see what smelled so good... and it did smell good. After it was cooked, I took some and put it on a plate for myself and the rest I put on a plate for him. It was piled up good. I took his plate and put it on the log at the edge of camp then went over and sat down on the cooler and started to eat. I took a bite and said, "Man, that's good. Go on... try it."

He picked up the plate and, with his fingers, ate the food and licked the plate. "Well, I guess I don't have to wash that one, now do I?" He put the plate down on the log and walked over to the creek and got a drink. "I know it was a little dry," I said, "but that's how I like my eggs. I should've put some ketchup on it for you."

He came over and made some sounds like he was talking to me, then walked away, back into the swamp.

I loaded up the boat and was getting ready to go when I heard him making a whistle noise. I looked out into the swamp and he was standing there looking at me. We made eye contact and he turned and walked away, not looking back.

I stood there, watching him disappear into the woods and said to myself, 'I wonder where he got that from?'

I came back the next weekend, but he was nowhere to be found. I walked all over that swamp looking for him but he was gone... not even a foot print. I stayed the night and the next day. I put out all the food and went back to town.

I wasn't sure if I would ever see him again.

    At first, Mike's interactions appeared to involve little more than eating and a lot of one-sided conversation. But it didn't surprise me. A creature living in the wilderness with only its wits and brute strength available to ensure its survival would naturally spend the majority of its time consuming calories. Mike had intuitively made an important distinction: the way to this creature's heart was, apparently, through its very large stomach.

As long as he played by the rules, the creature appeared to tolerate Mike's presence, and perhaps even welcomed it. But the learning curve, as he would come to discover, was steep.

All summer long, I searched for him and he was nowhere to be found. I stopped bringing food - all I was feeding was bears and coons. Every weekend, I would go to the sandbar and look for tracks but there were none. The camp was getting overgrown from lack of use.

It was November, and it was getting a little cooler, so I decided to go to camp and do some cleaning up and chop some wood. I hadn't been there much the last few months, just stopping by long enough to look for him... not staying overnight.

I got the weed-eater and cut down all the weeds, raked them up, and by the end of the day, I had plenty of firewood cut. I built a high table that he could eat off of so I didn't have to put his food on the ground and he could reach it better - that is, if he came back.

It was getting dark, so I loaded the boat and was getting ready to leave. I took one last look around. That's when I heard it. That scream - that wonderful scream that used to bring chills but was now music to my ears. "He's back! Snapperhead is back!" I yelled back and ran to my boat, got my pack and what food I had, strapped my pistol on and - without thinking - ran into the swamp.

I could hear him scream once in a while and I would answer. It was dark now and I was about a mile from camp. Reaching into my pack for my flashlight, I realized that in my rush I had forgotten it. I couldn't see much. When it gets dark in the swamp, it's dark.

The moon would be up soon, so I dug in and waited. I could hear something out there in the dark but I couldn't see what it was. I called out, "Are you there, Snapperhead?" He could have been right in front of me and I wouldn't have known it. I had an uneasy feeling that something wasn't right. I shouldn't have run out half-cocked. I should have waited in camp.

I sat there for about four hours until the moon was up and I could see a little. I started making my way back to camp. I was talking to myself, pissed that I had made a mistake like that. Who the hell did I think I was? Tarzan? I knew better than that. When you're all alone in a swamp and nobody knows where you are, you have to use your head. You get hurt and you can't just call 911. You break a leg or get snake bit and you're on your own.

About halfway to camp, I heard something coming up behind me. I stepped behind a tree and tried to see what it was. "Hey, buddy... is that you?" I said. "Come on... let me know you're there."

I didn't hear a sound. It was dead quiet - so quiet that my ears were ringing and I could hear my heart beating. That quiet. I strained my eyes, trying to see something. Anything. This wasn't right. Something was not right. I pulled my pistol, stepped out from behind the tree, and started walking back to camp.

That's when it hit me. Not an idea... a piece of wood, right in the back of the head.

I fell forward, face first in the mud. The pain was bad. I touched the back of my head and could feel the blood pouring out. I got to my feet and looked around and yelled, "What the hell is the matter with you? That hurt, you son of a bitch!" About that time, another piece came flying past my head. I couldn't see it, but I heard it as it flew by my ear. Then he screamed and hit me again. I turned and ran as fast as I could... when I was out of breath, I stopped. I could hear him out there and he kept throwing wood at me. I fired my gun up into the air and yelled, "That's the only warning you're going to get! The next one is coming your way, asshole!"

He hit me again. He was behind me, between me and the camp. Somehow, he had gotten around me or there was more than one.

I was hurting and bloody and said to myself, 'Now what are you going to do?' I reloaded my pistol and muttered, "Surprise attack, surprise attack. But he knows your here. Yes, but he doesn't know I'm going to attack him without mercy. There's nothing more surprising than an attack without mercy." I got that from a movie... I always wanted to say that. I was making jokes; trying to stay calm.

I could see a large shadow in front of me and I knew it was him, standing in the middle of the trail about fifty feet away. I yelled and ran right at him, shooting up in the air. He jumped out of the way and let me go by and I was sure glad he did... I had no backup plan. I mean, what would I do if he didn't move? Run into him? I wasn't going to shoot him.

He chased me all the way back to camp. (Or, on hindsight, he was "herding" me. He could have had me at any time.) When I got to camp, I was going to jump in my boat and take off but he was right on my tail, so I kept running along the creek bank. I had a quarter of a mile to go before I would get to the river and the sandbar. I didn't know if I could run that far, but with a Skunk Ape chasing you, you can do lots of things you never thought you could.

I made it to the river, busting out of the woods into the open. I ran out on the sand bar to the edge of the water. I looked at that black water and thought, I ain't jumping in there. No way.

I dropped to my knees and reloaded. I decided to make a stand there. I slammed the cylinder shut on my .44 mag and took aim. He was just coming out of the woods onto the bar. "Don't make me do this!" I yelled. "Back off! I don't want to hurt you!" But he kept coming, walking slowly toward me.

I stood up and cocked the hammer back. "Well," I said, "I guess they'll get their proof... their dead body... maybe something good will come from this."

He was twenty feet away and I felt my finger tighten on the trigger. Then I heard a growl from the edge of the woods to my right. I looked over and saw another swamp ape running down the bar, growling and making a fuss. The one in front of me turned and ran back into the woods. I turned and drew down on the second one and he stopped dead in his tracks.

He looked at me and walked back toward the woods. Stopping at the edge of the woods, he turned and slapped his chest and disappeared into the trees.

I sat down in the sand, shaking and out of breath. I lay on my back looking up at the moon. Did I just see that? My buddy saving my sorry ass? And the chest slap... Did he understand?

And who the hell was that jackass and what was his problem? I almost killed his ass. I wonder if he knows how close he came to being dead... And what about me? What the hell am I doing here?

I had to do some thinking.

I drifted off to sleep and was awoken by the Florida sun burning my face. I sat up and looked around. Hey, I didn't die. That's always a plus... I got to my feet and leaned down to pick up my pistol, half buried in the sand. That's nice... drop your gun in the sand. I froze at what I saw.

Footprints, all around me. Big footprints.

He had come back to check up on me and had sat down next to me, perhaps protecting me. I followed his tracks to the woods and made my way back to my boat.

When I'd fallen down that first time, I lost my hat - and I loved that hat - so I grabbed my shotgun and went to get it. When I got to the spot where I was knocked down, there it was in the middle of the trail. But that's not all. In the mud, there were baby Skunk Ape tracks. I put my foot on one and it was about the same size as my foot. Was that why that one went nuts? Was it protecting its young? If you think about it, a bear will do the same thing. The only difference is a bear would probably kill you if you got too close to her young. This one didn't want to kill me - it just wanted me to go away. That tells me that they are smarter than we give them credit for, because it could have killed me any time it wanted.

I went back to my boat and got a jug of water, washed the blood off me and cleaned up a bit.

After all, I can't go into town looking like I just got my ass beat by a Skunk Ape, now can I?

-8-

SURVIVAL OF THE FITTEST

As I read Mike's missive, a part of me felt understandably incredulous. Here was a man who reported experiences far beyond those of even the most intense of long-term witness cases I'd investigated.

It's imperative at this point in the story for me to address this, because I'm sure you will be asking yourself many of the same questions that I did.

I've always made it a point in my research to remain open-minded, yet skeptical. "Skepticism", nowadays, has become synonymous with summarily dismissing anything that doesn't jibe with common conceptions or popular belief. That isn't the kind of skepticism I mean. In my mind, good research requires listening and reserving judgment (you'll notice I emphasize this point often) while asking tough questions and analyzing the facts unemotionally. The key, I believe, is equanimity. Believers, whether they believe *in* the existence of something or the lack thereof, tend to be very emotional about their beliefs. A truly empirical and scientific approach does not *want* a particular thing to be true. It simply seeks what *is*.

However, being *coldly* scientific doesn't cut it either. There is a human element to be considered, not only in working with eyewitnesses but also in Bigfoot research in general. The trick is finding the balance.

In all the years I've spent interviewing eyewitnesses, I've learned a thing or two. Let's return, for a moment, to the difference between fact and interpretation. Witnesses are prone to interpreting facts via their own individual understanding of the world and what comes out of their mouth is often a heavily biased interpretation of events.

For instance, a witness will tell me, "Bigfoot banged on the side of our house last night." They may even go so far as to say, "I think he wanted to let us know that he was angry because we fenced-in the garden." Notice the interpretation? When questioned by an astute investigator, the FACT is that the witness simply heard a couple of thumps on the side of their house at about 11:00 p.m. the previous evening. That's the fact.

Another thing I've learned is that witnesses who fabricate stories usually start out simple and begin to embellish as they progress, or as further questions are asked. When forced to make something up on the fly in order to answer a question, they can rarely keep their story straight. A story told more than once will generally begin to include embellishments not originally included – *or even alluded to* - in the original story. This is a crucial key in determining credibility.

My awareness of this has become somewhat second nature to me when interviewing witnesses. I don't think about these things consciously during an interview - I'll simply let the witness talk, note any red flags that might come up, perhaps ask additional questions, and then move on... saving the real digestion of all of the information until the interview is over. This serves two important purposes: First, it allows me to focus on what the witness is saying. Secondly, by reserving judgment and interacting with the witness as such, he or she feels more comfortable and is more willing to share all that they know. In a case where a witness is deliberately lying, they're convinced that you're "buying" their story and will tend to let their guard down, making it easier to spot discrepancies in the telling.

When Mike and I began talking on the phone, he was reserved. He alluded to certain experiences in conversation, but didn't offer any details then. As we continued talking, and his trust in me grew, I began to notice something different about Mike as a witness. He rarely interpreted anything. He simply told me what happened, what he saw, what he heard, what he thought at the time, how he felt... Occasionally he would ask a question about the behaviors he observed (such as in the encounter he described above, wondering if the aggression was due to its young being in the vicinity), but he rarely came to any firm conclusions or harbored any "opinions" or "theories" about the creatures. He was, as he continually reminded me, "no expert".

The other thing I found compelling was that Mike would allude to something in conversation, sometimes almost off-handedly, and then back off from the subject just as quickly. "I might tell you about that later," he'd say.

When "later" would come, and he would tell me the full details of that particular encounter, I would think back to the conversation we'd had and the context in which he had briefly mentioned the event. And I would suddenly understand why he had mentioned it in that context... and why he had been reluctant to tell me more at that time. (This has happened more times than I can count – and is still occurring as Mike continues to open up.)

As our trust for one another grew and our conversations became more candid, he would often refer *back* to encounters he'd already related to me, in passing and in the normal course of conversation. These references were always fully in context and their introduction into the conversation never felt contrived or deliberate. He was simply mentioning something pertaining to what we were discussing. If I asked him to elaborate again, he would, the details of the story never faltering from those I'd heard before. On rare occasions, he would remember a detail he'd failed to mention. Upon relating it, he would emphasize the fact that he had just remembered it, somewhat embarrassed, muttering about getting old and memory loss - in other words, he knew he couldn't have shared that detail with me previously because he'd forgotten it until just then.

   In order for Mike to have concocted this story, he would have had to have fabricated multiple, detailed interactions long before we began talking and had the presence of mind to allude to certain ones long before the actual telling took place. There was never a hint of sensationalism or boastfulness in Mike's recounting of the events. On the contrary, he often expressed reluctance to relate a particular encounter, saying, "You probably won't believe me..." Often, he tentatively began a story with the words, "This is hard for me to talk about..." He not only wanted NO publicity, he was adamant about my keeping his name and location strictly confidential.

   The details he related meshed with things I had surmised over the years about these creatures' nature and behavior. The subtle details he related, and his intimate understanding and knowledge of this subject left me with only two conclusions. Either Mike had studied this subject as intensely as I had, for as *long* as I had, and accumulated that knowledge expressly for the purpose of fabricating an unprecedented number of detailed interactions and chose *me* to as the recipient of one of the greatest hoaxes of all time... and to what purpose?

   Or he really had experienced all of this.

    As I've come to know him, I've realized that although he is a very intelligent man, Mike doesn't strike me as someone who is particularly "creative".

When he came back that time, after being gone all summer, he had others with him. [Notice that Mike alludes to this here in this first part of the missive. Carefully re-reading his initial emails to me, I noted subtle references to more than one creature. The details about the "others" would come later.]

He would still come around but wouldn't stay long. He would eat and take as much as he could with him, so I didn't see him as much as I used to. I think he had other things to worry about. Maybe he had a family to look after.

That winter, I only saw him once or twice a month. I was out of town working a lot and it was hard to get back, as much as I wanted to. And after that night, I wasn't as willing to go out there... It took me a while to get past it. I guess it made me take a hard look at what I was doing.

I thought that my interfering with him was doing more harm than good. I had become a food source and I was afraid he would walk up to other people, like a hunter, and get shot. So I stopped bringing as much food around. I still fed him - just not as much.

    By the time I got to this point in Mike's story, I was a little confused. Over the phone, he had stressed to me that this creature was more like a person than an animal. But the way Mike was describing him here, it was as if he was talking about feeding a wild animal.

Mike was sharing his understanding of this creature at the time. As his experiences continued, his perception evolved. Mike would come to realize that he didn't have to worry about this creature perceiving all humans in the same way.

I would follow him around to see what he did all day. I had to stay far away so that whatever he did had nothing to do with me. And let me tell you... he did some things you would not believe...

Here, Mike begins a sort of free-form, rambling diatribe with some of his signature humor thrown in, trying to share as many of the things he'd witnessed over the years as he could think of.

He will eat just about anything. If he can chase it down and knock it in the head, he will eat it.

He would pick up a piece of wood, throw it at a bird, run up, and grab it. If it was not already dead, he would pull its head off. Then, he would pull most of the feathers off and eat the whole thing. It was hard to watch - it made me want to puke.

He also liked turtles. He would pick one up and pull the shell apart - you can hear the shell crack like a big walnut - then eat it like we eat oysters on the half shell.

He would chase coons up trees and then push on the tree to make it fall out. Sometimes, the tree would fall over and the coon would hit the ground running. Sometimes they got away - most times, not. Do you really want me to tell you how he eats a coon? First, he pulls the head off, and then he pulls the hide off. This only takes a few seconds to do. Then he pulls the legs off one at a time and eats them. By now, the guts are hanging down and he pulls them out. He don't eat them - only the meat.

Now, as you might guess, he gets it all over himself and I think that's where some of the smell comes from, because sometimes he smells like a dead animal and I can't stand to be around him. I put Vicks [Vaporub] in my mustache to help counter the smell. He don't always smell that bad, but he does get extra ripe sometimes and I have to stay upwind. And when he takes a crap, he squats down and lets fly. Trust me, it don't smell no better: don't plan on eating a big supper after a day with the Big Guy.

Fish: depending on what kind it is, he just eats them whole like we eat a hot dog. But that's only fish that don't have scales like catfish and eels. If it has scales, he rips it open and eats down to the scales like we eat smoked mullet, from the inside out, throwing the scales away.

He will hide behind a tree with a big stick about as big around as a baseball bat - only longer - and wait for a wild pig to walk by and then he whacks the pig on the head and kills it. He eats a pig the same way he eats a coon, only he leaves the head on the pig.

I have seen him take a log and pull it apart to get at the grubs inside. Bears do the same thing, but bears have claws to help. Skunk Apes only have their fingers, and they can rip a log apart in just a short time. "Strong" is not the word to describe how powerful this guy is. Clyde ain't got nothing on this guy - screw the Caddy… he could scrap an eighteen-wheeler with his bare hands in no time at all.

Oh, and let's not forget farts… Skunk Ape farts are in a class all by themselves. He will be standing there and let one rip, then he'll look around like he don't know where it came from. Trust me on this one: if a Skunk Ape asks you to pull his finger, don't do it.

What else have I forgotten? Oh, yeah... big feet, big Johnson. Never seen one hard, thank God, but if I ever did I think I would run screaming into the night. But all joking aside, with all the hair you can't really see it. In Florida, you need to have a permit to carry a concealed weapon...

I'm sure I am leaving out a lot of stuff... like roots. He eats roots and swamp cabbage, which is the heart of a cabbage palm. I have to use a chainsaw or axe to get a swamp cabbage but he can rip one out of a tree in no time.

Frogs... he likes frogs. One frog, one bite - enough said about frogs.

Hunters turn their deer dogs loose to run deer... I saw him chase a Walker deer dog one day. The poor dog was so scared, he ran off a ten-foot bank and landed about thirty feet out in the river to get away. I got my boat and fished him out before a gator got him. He was shaking so hard, I thought he was going to die. I found him a good home, but his deer-chasing days were over.

And to show how smart he is... The locals put out trott lines to catch catfish. He must have seen them do it because he will pull their lines out of the water and take the fish. When the fishermen come back to check their lines, all they get is a tangled mess. They think other people are doing it because they have asked me if I saw anything. He also does the same thing with eel traps: he pulls the trap, tears it open and eats the eels.

Despite the humorous overtones in Mike's description of the Skunk Ape's diet, behavior and physical attributes, he emphasizes once again here the raw, primal nature of these creatures and their focus on survival. Table manners and couth do not appear to be high on the list of a Skunk Ape's priorities.

But this got me thinking: Why should they? These creatures find what they need and do what they have to in order to survive. How very, very different they are from us in that respect.

We humans started out as hunters and gatherers as well. The difference was, we weren't nearly so well equipped to begin with. So we developed the use of tools and fire, and began to make things we needed to ensure our survival.

We feared cold, so we killed animals for their hides and built fires to keep our little hairless bodies warm. We feared hunger, so we ate their flesh and began using sticks and rocks to dig for roots because our hands weren't strong enough to do the job for us. We feared thirst, so we learned to create water reservoirs from animal bladders to ensure we could carry water where there was none. We feared the dark, and our eyes didn't work well at night, so we carried torches or stayed inside when the sun went down. We feared predators, so we made weapons to even out the playing field. We feared the elements, so we used our tools to create shelter.

Along came invention, agriculture, and industry. Suddenly, all of the things we desperately needed to ensure our survival became easier to use, easier to acquire. We became obsessed with convenience. Animal furs made way for mass-produced textiles. Our clothing got dirty, so we invented the washing machine. Other people began growing and killing our food for us, so we started working in textile mills or washing machine factories to acquire money to buy our food. Big Macs replaced hunks of fresh venison roasted on a stick over a fire, and as long as you had a job, even at McDonald's, you were pretty much ensured the means for a place to live, food to eat, clothes to wear, water to drink... We moved into the valleys, away from the wilderness, and built concrete and glass civilizations where every amenity was a phone call or car ride away. The internet came along, ensuring access to anything in the world our hearts could desire, as long as we could point and click and had a credit card handy.

For us, employment equals survival. It's no wonder our world swiftly goes to hell in a hand basket when the job market fails.

But something else happened, too. We became lazy. We developed feelings of entitlement. We became over-stimulated and easily bored. Somewhere along the way, we stopped creating because we needed to, and began making stuff simply because we *could*, purely for entertainment. Millions of Billy the Bass wall plaques clog our landfills while strains of "Take Me To The River" waft on the breeze. Reality TV devours the documentary genre while we sit glued to our television sets, our collective behinds getting fatter by the day, entertained but hardly educated.

The biggest thing we appear to fear now is *boredom*.

We are constantly inundated by people trying to sell us the things they make. We're bombarded by advertisements, telling us we aren't tan enough, tall enough, thin enough, rich enough, our teeth aren't white enough... We live in an alien civilization of glass and concrete, plastic money and fashion trends, far removed from the natural world. We have become dependent upon artifacts, obsessed with artifice, highly "sophisticated", both technologically and culturally...

And very, very vulnerable.

If the electrical grid fails for good tomorrow, can we survive without our refrigerators? Do we know how to fish, how to hunt, how to create things necessary for our survival, without a fully stocked Wal-Mart within driving distance to supply the tools, the duct tape, the needles and thread? Will we know how to cure meat or tan a hide? How many of us will find ourselves running to our computers to search the internet for the answers, only to find that our connection to that vast storehouse of knowledge is *gone*... and simple survival, once again, is the sole focus of our lives?

Is this what it means, then, to be "human"?

Sasquatches didn't need tools or weapons - their strength was sufficient. They didn't need clothing - they were already covered with hair. They didn't need fire - they can apparently digest raw meat just fine. They didn't need light - their vision allows them to see in the dark. They live as they have lived, perhaps for millions of years, creating nothing, wanting for nothing.

And we wonder why it's so very difficult for us to discover them? To find something, we must first *understand* it. How can we inherently understand something that lives in a world so far removed from the one we've created for ourselves?

A great debate rages in the research community whether these creatures are "animal" or "human", whether they are "intelligent"... and, if so, how intelligent?

I suppose it depends upon how one defines intelligence. We humans pat ourselves on the back for being so intelligent. We're great at creating things we need. We also create things we don't need, screwing up the environment and shitting in our nests - so to speak - in the process. Everything we make is made from something. In other words, everything we create *destroys* something else. We sit on the john and wipe our behinds with trees, reading newspapers made of trees, in houses made of trees.

Meanwhile, Sasquatch simply live amongst the trees. (At least, the ones we haven't cut down to wipe with.)

We create and destroy, destroy and create, wantonly and indiscriminately, for comfort, for pleasure, for entertainment, as we slowly become increasingly dependent upon our creations.

Is that intelligence?

One definition of intelligence is "the capacity to acquire and apply knowledge." But our perception of intelligence has, over the years, perhaps taken on a more sociocentric tone.

Imagine, for a moment, two men standing side-by-side.

William is a Harvard Graduate and a professor of law. He's dressed in a natty three-piece suit, is articulate, well groomed, tall, tan, and athletic, has a blindingly white smile and is financially successful.

Troy stands beside him. He is a third-generation fisherman from the bayou and grew up wrestling 'gators. He wears a flannel shirt, filthy overalls, has a bit of a paunch, murders proper English with a slow drawl, is missing a couple of teeth and spits on the sidewalk in between sentences.

At first glance, which of these men do you believe most people would perceive to be more "intelligent"?

Sophistication has become synonymous with intelligence. But take William to a swamp and leave him there... and you'll quickly discover that intelligence is entirely relative.

Poor William wouldn't have a clue how to survive.

Can you shave a Bigfoot, stick him in a three-piece suit, invite him to dinner and expect him to blend in? No. But does his lack of what we consider "culture" and "manners" preclude him from having the capacity to acquire and apply knowledge?

No.

Intelligence is only one part of the equation. Do Skunk Apes, or Sasquatches, possess other qualities that would cause us to perceive them as being more "human" than animal? Or are they simply big, stinky, crude, mindless eating machines?

Mike was about to shed a little light on that subject as well.

–9–

THE NATURE OF THE BEAST

One day, I was walking along the main river and came across a bunch of people across the river on another sandbar, swimming and having a family-and-friends day. I could smell the Bar-B-Q. There were around twenty-five or so - kids to grownups - and they were having a good time, whooping and hollering, music playing... Good times, good times. There were eight, maybe ten, people swimming and they were floating on tubes.

I was standing in the trees watching them having fun and wondering if they knew how lucky they were, having family and friends who cared about them. I've never had that and never will, but I'll bet it's a great feeling.

I sat down, leaned against a tree, and took it all in, thinking about my own life and wishing things had been different. I would have liked to have had a wife and kids but it just wasn't in the cards for me. (I like kids... in fact, I tell people that I get along great with kids and dogs. It's everyone else that I have problems with.)

As I was sitting there, I heard something walking behind me. I looked around and it was the Big Guy. I guess he heard the noise and came to see what was going on. (That's what they do: they like to know who's in the neighborhood and will come and see.) He was up from me about thirty feet and was looking across the *river. I didn't say anything; I just waited to see what he would do.*

I thought that he would leave after he saw who it was, but he just stood there watching them. After a while, one of the kids was playing around and pushed one of the tubes with a girl about seven or eight years old out into the current. It took off downriver - not fast, but faster than they could swim. She was screaming for someone to come get her, and started to cry. She was in no real danger as long as she stayed on the tube but she was scared just the same.

She floated past us and the Big Guy got real nervous and started walking downriver, following her. He never took his eyes off her. As he came past me, I said, "She'll be ok. Look, they got the boat to go get her." But he had a worried look on his face and was making a whimpering sound and kept going.

The boat came flying by, picked her up, and took her back to her mom. He came back and took up his spot and kept watching them. After a bit, he sat down and we stayed there all afternoon.

I was thinking what a sorry pair we were. I think we felt the same way. But he showed a real concern for that little girl. I wonder if he would have tried to save her.

(You never know when you're being watched and I bet those people would have freaked out if they knew a Skunk Ape and his sidekick were watching them.)

The sun was going down and the people went home. The Big Guy walked into the woods and did not even say goodbye. He acted like he was sad.

I made my way back to camp and started a fire and was cooking supper when he came up, looking like he'd lost his best friend. I said, "What's wrong? You feeling lonesome? Tell me all about it..." He just stood there looking at me. I looked at him holding my arms out and said, "What? Are you gonna just stand there and stare at me? Are you hungry? Here... try this."

I opened a can of Spam and gave it to him. He sniffed it, then licked it, then took a bite. His eyes got real wide and he put the rest in his mouth. He loved it. I told him, "You had that before, just not out of the can... but it's good, ain't it? I'll make a Cracker out of you yet... you wait and see."

I gave him some fruit and bread. He ate, and then went into the swamp and I didn't see him the rest of that night.

The next day, it was raining so I headed back to town. I felt bad for leaving him but I had to go back to work and it was a nine-hour drive, so I wanted to get going before it got too late. I left him the rest of the food, like I always do. I didn't get to see him before I went and felt bad about going. I'm sure he saw me go...

I think he always knows when I come and go even when I don't see him. I always yell, "Gotta go, Big Guy! Smell ya later! There's food on the table for ya!" Then I get in the boat and go, always looking for him on the way out. Sometimes he'll come down to the river to see me off.

Compassion. Concern. Mike's Skunk Ape had appeared worried about the little girl on the river. But did that mean that this creature was capable of thoughtful compassion, or was its reaction simply instinctual - like an animal's? The "human or animal" question had bothered me for as long as I could remember. I felt that figuring out where these creatures lay within the gradient of black and white between the two was paramount to understanding their nature. I hoped that Mike would continue to shed some light on this. Despite the fact that he had no idea what questions I'd been asking all these years, his experiences seemed to provide the answers.

When I look into his eyes, I almost expect him to talk. It's like looking into a human's eyes. You can tell there's something more there. A knowing a look of wisdom, and a sadness - like a longing for something from long ago.

He would sometimes sit and look out into the swamp or across the river like he was waiting for someone. Maybe a lost love or one of his own kind - a familiar face, someone he could relate to. Can you imagine what it's like to be the only one of your kind around for miles and having no contact? Not having that sense of belonging to someone to make your life full and meaningful?

He would stare out into the night and you could tell that his thoughts were far away. And once in a while, he would let out a low and mournful howl and I could hear it echo through the swamp. Then, he would be quiet, as if waiting for a reply. It was really a sad sound and added an eerie feel to the night.

 Early on, the creature always appeared alone, and Mike assumed that he was the only Skunk Ape around for miles. It wasn't until later that he'd discovered that there were others.

I think he has a way of knowing what I'm feeling... it's like he can sense my mood and he responds to whatever I'm feeling at that time. I've noticed that when I'm in a depressed state of mind he stays closer to me. He will come into camp at night and stare at me when he thinks I'm asleep, the way you would check on a child late at night, making sure everything's okay. But when I'm upbeat and feeling good, he acts more like the man next door. You say hello, you bullshit awhile, then you go on about your own thing, knowing the other one is there and only a few steps away if you need something.

I think that might be why he comes around me... we feel the same way and he picks up on it. He can relate to me like I would understand the way he feels.

But in the spring, things change. He doesn't come around as much and I can hear other swamp apes out in the swamp and across the river. I see more shadows moving around at night and I can hear them calling to one another.

I hear people say Skunk Apes tree knock, but I have never heard it. I am not saying they don't do it, but I think it could be used as a covert way for them to let each other know when humans are around. Think about it... if you don't want to give away your position, you find a way to talk without doing it. In WWI or II, the soldiers had clickers. If you weren't sure who was making that noise sneaking around in the dark, you would use your clicker. If you clicked and got a click back, you knew it was another GI and you held your fire.

These wild humans, as I like to call them, are smart. They have the mental brass to do something like that. That's why you can't find them.

What are they? I've given it a lot of thought, after being around this one, seeing what he does and the way he acts. The way he can overcome and adapt to changes in his environment. The way he reacts to the presence of humans - hiding and watching from a distance, learning what we do. Knowing how to see the dangers we humans put on them, like cars and guns and highways, and staying out of harm's way. And teaching their young to stay away from humans and to watch out for the dangers.

This shows me that there is a high level of intelligence on their part. You can say that all animals have this and that Skunk Apes are no different from a deer or bobcat. But how many Skunk Apes are hit by cars and how many deer and bobcats are wiped out each year crossing the road? They know how to see danger and how to react to it, like stepping around a rattlesnake instead of on it. And how to kill it, and what part to beware of and what part they can eat, pulling off the head and throwing it away. How to get catfish off a hook and not getting hooked themselves. How to watch out for the mouth on a snapping turtle and how to get it before it gets them.

If you took a human child and put it in the woods, far away from other humans... if that child survived and you found it again ten years later... what would you find? Would you find a normal teenager? Or would you find a wild human, living off the land, not trusting humans, long forgetting that it, too, was human? Could it read and write? Could it speak? Would it understand the world of humans? Could it learn to do all the things we do? How would its brain develop? Would it stay wild forever or would it slowly return to what we call "civilized"?

Skunk Apes are a lot like that. They are more like a wild human than wild animal. They are a lot like us, only better... they don't prey on each other, and they share food and care for each other.

If you give a swamp ape food, he will share it with you. More than once, I have given the Big Guy a bag of apples or peaches, only to have him toss me one - and when I finished it, he would toss me another, until they were all gone. At first, he didn't do this. He would take it and run. But over time, after trust was built, he started sharing food with me. (You learn to eat it and like it, Skunk Ape spit and all. It can be gross at times... always have water close by to rinse it with. And only eat food that you brought... unless you like raw coon or turtle.)

A lot of wildlife comes out at night because it is safer than the daytime. Why? Because of humans. Humans will kill you, so you learn to hide and the cover of darkness is a good way to move around and not be seen. Skunk Apes know this and that's another reason they are hard to find. But they also come out in the daytime when there are no humans around. (Come to think of it, wildlife knows humans are bad news even on their best days, so they know to stay away.)

With all wildlife, finding food is their number one thing to do. Swamp apes are no different. As they move around, they are always feeding, eating whatever they can find.

I have seen him take off at a full run, chasing down a rabbit or some other small animal. He can run, I would guess, around thirty miles per hour... and that's from a dead stop. Just walking, I have to almost run to keep him in sight. He could cover well over forty miles in a day. He walks fast and deliberately when he needs to go somewhere. It's like he is on autopilot and lets nothing slow him down.

So if you have ever been chased by one and not gotten caught, he didn't want to catch you. You will not outrun one and if you are standing face to face with one, you belong to him. You won't get away if he wants you. The best thing to do is to stand still and be calm. (Good luck with that one. 'Calm' will be the last thing on your mind...)

But you might find that you are not as scared as you thought you'd be.

When you look into the eyes of a Skunk Ape, you'll know what mood he's in and if he's going to hurt you - just like a human. His eyes tell a story - all you have to do is read it and heed what it tells you. He'll let you know right now what he wants you to do, and if he wants you to run screaming into the night, you'd better do it.

Soon, your fear will be replaced by awe. Just the sight of him up close is going to make you run the full range of emotion, from fear to a feeling that you are in the presence of something as old as time. And you'll see a wisdom in his eyes that will take your breath away - if the smell hasn't already.

From my childhood sighting, I remembered that *look* in the eyes... that eerie depth and presence that told me I was looking at an intelligent creature. Those eyes caused me to spend my entire adult life seeking understanding.

*****

During one of our earlier conversations, Mike and I discussed aggression in Bigfoot sightings. I explained that most of the seeming acts of "aggression" I'd heard or read about, whether it was stomping, screaming, breaking-trees or throwing objects at humans, seemed to be *caused* by humans – either directly by their invasive and annoying behavior, or their mere presence in the woods in certain circumstances.

Mike got quiet. "You've gotta understand… There ain't no bunny rabbits and butterflies when it comes to this guy. If he sees you, you belong to him. You don't belong to your Momma no more. I could tell you about something that happened – but you won't believe me…"

"Mike," I said gently, "you haven't said anything yet that's really surprised me."

He took a deep breath. "Okay. But don't say I didn't warn you."

He related an unnerving and somewhat amusing encounter to me then, which he shared again now in his writings:

The most important thing I can tell you is this: Do not, under any circumstances, poke a Skunk Ape with a stick. They do not like this.

One day, I was feeling extra good and playful and had gotten used to being around him and started doing things that, in reflection, I should not have done.

He was sitting on the big log in my camp, eating a box of food I'd given him. He was really chowing down. I was sitting on the other end of the log about eight feet away from him.

I picked up a stick about six feet long and as big around as my thumb. I pulled all the twigs off it but left a couple of leaves at the end. I started tickling his ear with it and he would swat at it, like it was a fly. Then he saw it was me and turned and let out a cross between a huff and a growl.

Now, most people would take this as a hint to stop messing around... but, like I said, I was feeling playful on this day. So I stepped it up a notch and started poking him in the side with it - not hard, just a little - and I asked, "What's the matter, Big Guy... a little grumpy today?" and poked him again.

In the blink of an eye, he dropped the box of food and reached out and grabbed the stick and pulled me to him. It happened so fast that I didn't have time to let go. With his right hand, he grabbed me by the chest and, in one motion, stood up and threw me like a shot put over my boat into the creek.

I landed about five feet past my boat in the middle of the creek. I stood up - it was only about four feet deep - and looked up and he was standing at the edge of the water, stick in hand, switching it back and forth like he was swatting flies.

I yelled, "What the hell did you do that for, Snapperhead?" He just stood there with a smug look on his face, almost grinning.

I waded over to the creek bank and tried to get out but he would poke me with that stick and switch me with it. "Damn it, that hurts! Now, knock it off! I get your point... Don't poke you with a stick, right?" But every time I tried to climb out, he would poke me and switch me.

Backing up I said, "Look... there are baby gators in here and the mothership won't be far off, so let me out before you get me gator-caught." I don't think he cared if I got gator-caught. He just *stood there with that stick.* "Okay... I will use my super-human brain to out smart you..." *I waded over to my boat and was going to climb up on it. I put my hands on the gunnel and was about hop up on it when he grabbed it with one hand and pulled the boat out of the water and up on the bank.*

I couldn't believe what I just saw. "Now what the hell did you do that for?" *He stood there with that stick he had, with an okay-jackass-it's-your-move look in his eyes.*

I sat down with only my head above water. "Okay. You win. I'm sorry... I won't poke you with no damn stick no more." *He dropped the stick, went back to the log, sat down, and started eating.*

I climbed out of the creek and looked at my boat. "You're gonna help me put it back in the water, right?"

He grunted, which I took as a no, so I went over and sat down on the log, staring at my boat. I said, "That's cold, man. Really cold." *He pulled an apple from the box and handed it to me.*

When he finished eating, he got up and started walking off into the swamp. I yelled after him, "Okay, so I guess I'll just have to refloat the boat by myself. Is that what you're telling me?"

He snorted over his shoulder and kept walking.

I think I really pissed him off, but I think we bonded that day, too. It's one of my favorite memories of all. On the other hand, it was a reminder of how powerful he is and that I should be more careful around him. Sometimes I forget who he is and treat him like a pet. That whole thing could've ended a lot differently.

As our friendship progressed and Mike shared more about his personal life and experiences, I began to understand what he called the "Perfect Storm" of circumstances that caused him to achieve what so many of us have tried and failed - intimate interaction with and understanding of these creatures.

At the time he was working on the river, and happened to see the tracks, Mike was going through a difficult period in his life. Like so many of us who experience emotional pain, he sought solace where he could find it. For Mike, it was the solitude of the swamp. As the human world continued to frustrate and disappoint him, the natural world beckoned. Here, there was silence - a place to think, to escape, to center himself, without the pressures of society and conformity. For a time, the pain was so great that Mike spent nearly all of his time in the swamp, avoiding people... and living like a Skunk Ape.

At first, the elusive, shadowy form that quietly shared his retreat presented a welcome distraction. The challenge of chasing a Skunk Ape through the cypress trees was preferable to sitting quietly and feeling the past encroach upon him. But as Mike's visits to the swamp lengthened, so did his understanding of - and relationship with - this creature.

Mike explains, "I was out there for personal reasons that had nothing to do with finding a Skunk Ape. That's the difference between me and all of those tree-knockers. I wasn't out to prove anything to anybody."

It made sense. Here was a guy who was practically *living* in the swamp, who felt he had little to lose, who had pretty much divorced himself from humanity. He moved into a Skunk Ape's backyard, had no agenda besides simple curiosity, developed a rapport with a creature which would eventually become something akin to a friendship... and found himself healing in the process. And he wasn't going to tell anyone about it, because the last thing he wanted to do was bring harm to the companion who had been with him through one of the worst times of his life.

−10−

NOT JUST A PRETTY FACE

J umping back to when I first started to see him on a regular basis: He would let me leave food for him but wouldn't come to get it until I had moved far off. This was when I still had to watch him through field glasses.

I had left some food at this spot where the sun broke through the trees and the ground was drier than the rest of the swamp. It was the only place where pines grew and the pine needles covered the ground like a carpet. He would sit down and eat. Sometimes, after eating, he would lay down on the pine needles and sleep.

One day, he had been sleeping for about an hour and I was looking around the swamp to see what else was out there. I saw some movement to the north of me and was trying to make out what it was.

Hunters.

It was hunters - four of them, making their way through the swamp. They all had rifles and were heading straight for the spot where the Big Guy was sleeping. This was not good... If they walked up on him, they would shoot him for sure.

I looked over to where the Big Guy was sleeping and he was kneeling down behind some bushes, watching the hunters come toward him. Somehow, he knew they were there and was hiding to see what they were going to do. I don't know if he heard them or smelled them, but he knew they were coming and he was on full alert. It was unfolding right in front of me.

I waited to see what he would do. I reloaded my shotgun with slugs and was going to back him up if he needed it. I was not going to shoot anyone... just shoot at them to give them something else to think about other than the Swamp Ape, and give him time to get away.

What he did next was so cool that it made me laugh. He just stepped to one side and let them pass. He moved so fast, staying close to the ground, that he looked more like a bear than a swamp ape, moving along the ground and ducking into some bushes about seventy-five feet from where he had been sleeping. He waited for the hunters to go past, hiding in that bush. They never even knew he was there.

After they passed, he went the other way, moving quickly, looking over his shoulder as he went. I would've thought he would have run away from them but he did what I would have done... he hid and let them pass, and then went back the way they had come. That was a smart move on his part and showed me that he was not just a pretty face.

He knew they were a danger to him and got as far away as fast as he could. I watched him as long as I could and, like a puff of smoke, he was gone. I didn't see him again for almost a month.

The hunters were wearing full camouflage and it was hard for me to see them at first, but he knew. They didn't fool him; he saw them coming and they never had a clue he was there.

Again, here was Mike - the Skunk Ape's sidekick, as it were - watching people in the swamp not from a human's perspective, but *from that of a Skunk Ape*. The elusive behavior he described witnessing was clever. And completely expected. How else would something avoid humans for so long unless it had gotten very, very good at it? Moving in the direction that they had *come from* not only ensured that he would not run into them; it also put twice as much distance between him and the hunters.

But something else struck me about this particular incident: We're cautioned not to feed animals in the wild because they tend to become habituated to humans and will approach humans indiscriminately, looking for the next handout. "Nuisance" bears often have to be trapped and relocated when they become accustomed to being fed by campers or well-meaning rural neighbors. But the Skunk Ape apparently knew the difference between Mike and other humans. Rather than approaching the hunters for food, he hid, then fled.

I was nearing the end of this incredible account. As I read Mike discussing what, to him, seemed to be rather mundane details of a Skunk Ape's behavior and appearance, I couldn't help but grin. Thinking of those who had spent so many years interviewing witness after witness who'd merely watched a Bigfoot cross the road, I imagined the incredulity on the faces of those researchers if they were to read details like these. Would they believe it?

Ironically, probably not.

People have reported that Bigfoot was watching them, peeking in their windows, walking on their porch, watching them from the woods while they were working in the fields or logging. They want to know about us. It's only natural that they would.

I've seen him follow a boat that was drifting downriver. The men in it who were fishing were unaware that they were being studied.

I have also seen him climb onto the lighters that local hunters and fishermen tie up along the riverbanks. (A lighter is a houseboat that doesn't have an engine and has to be towed - it's an old Cracker word you don't hear much anymore.) He will climb on these lighters, look around, and peek in the windows. Some are so small that he almost turns them over climbing on board. He pulled one loose from the tree it was tied to and I had to run and get my boat and tow it back.

He is a good swimmer. He wades out until he can't touch bottom and then dog paddles the rest of the way. It doesn't take him long to cross the river.

He smells better after he dries and his hair is more red in color... maybe it washes the dirt off him and the real color comes out. Also, I've noticed that when it rains, the water dripping off him is black from the mud and dirt.

The first time he really let me touch him, I reached out my hand and touched his. It felt rough, like a piece of old leather: soft, but tough. Then I put my hand on his arm and felt his hair. It was stiff and bristly, like hair gets when it's not washed. Afterward, I smelled my hand and it smelled no worse than if I had been petting a dog. I thought it would stink but it didn't - which brings me to another thought about his smell... I wonder if he has scent glands that secrete an odor of some kind - maybe to attract a mate - because sometimes he doesn't really smell that bad.

He will lie in the sun until he gets hot, then he goes and lays in the shade to cool off, and he'll repeat it over and over again. Solar fix... that's what I call it. I don't know why he does it, but when I was a kid I used to do the same thing: lay out in the sun. Not to get tan, but because the sun felt so good. Maybe I have some Skunk Ape in me. I'd better shake my family tree to see if any Skunk Apes fall out.

It was almost finished. I felt strange... somehow deeply fulfilled, but disappointed at the same time. I had so many questions left unanswered... then, something caught my eye that told me that I probably hadn't even heard the half of it...

There are others.

They don't let me get close, but I can see them moving around and they won't come into camp. I know they come up at night and check me out. I can hear them walking all around me and if I walk toward them they are gone. If I had the time, I think I could bring them in. I would have to buy a lot of food.

Once in a while, one will throw something into camp and I'll stand up and say, "Hey! Knock that crap off!"

I got to thinking one night: Have you seen people go to the zoo? They walk up to a cage and the animal is laying down, but people want to see it do something... so they will throw a peanut or something at it to make it move. Or they will see a gator sunning on the bank, asleep, and they will throw something at it to make it move. People want to be entertained and a sleeping lion or gator ain't no fun.

Maybe they throw stuff at me to make me move so they can be entertained. It would not surprise me one bit... they are so much like us.

You will find that as we want to know about them, they want to know about us, and as time goes on, if people will let them be and stop chasing them around the woods, they will let themselves be known to certain people that they feel they can trust. They aren't going to come around you if you pursue them. When you chase something, it only makes it mistrust you even more. In the wild, if you are being chased, you know that if you get caught you will be killed - so that alone will make you run faster. So if you're a Skunk Ape and a thousand yogurt-eaters are chasing you, trying to take your photo... what are you going to do? They don't know that you only want to take their photo. They think you want to hurt them, so they'll stay away from you.

The only way to find a Skunk Ape is to let him find you. They can tell if you're trouble or not. You wouldn't walk into a biker bar if you weren't a biker, would you? And why not? Because you know that you'll be in danger of getting your ass kicked. And that's why, if you chase them, they run away and hide. They know you're trouble. And the more people chase them, the less they will trust humans and the longer it will take to make the kind of contact that I have with this one.

I let him know that I was not a threat; I let him know that I was in the area. I let him come to me. But this was after I chased him around the swamp for four years getting nowhere. One day, I got it: let him come to me if he wants to. A year later, he did. He watched me for a long time before I could even get a distant look at him. When I would point a camera at him, he'd get spooked and pissed off. Anything that isn't natural, he sees as a threat.

So now, I'm to the point that I want to protect him and get laws passed to protect him and his kind from humans who want to kill them. I need to prove that he is there but to do so puts him in danger. I'm damned if I do, and damned if I don't. If I tell where he is, people will come and I know what will happen... It would be like letting a child molester into a daycare. So what do I do? Take the risk and expose him? He would be the only one at risk... not me. So what right do I have to do that to him? Would you put your own child at risk to prove a point or would you do what's best for the child?

Many times over the years, he's had many close calls with hunters - and I've noticed that when people are in the swamp he will not walk along the trails. He's always off to one side, choosing to stay in the areas most people won't walk. People will always take the easy way and stay on the trails and that's why they don't find as many tracks. He'll go out of his way to stay out of sight, always choosing the paths where there are no paths.

Most researchers won't wade ass-deep into a swamp... or even ankle deep. They're afraid of the swamps and woods and what's in them. Most of them are cubical-dwelling yogurt-eaters who couldn't find a Skunk Ape if he was in their backyard. I know that sounds bad, but they're the problem and they can't see it. Everyone needs to stop chasing them, sit down, and wait. They will find you, if you are worthy in their eyes.

If you are not a good person and put out bad vibes, he will pick up on it and you'll only see where he has been. My point is this: if you meet someone and he makes you feel uneasy, you'll most likely get away from him as fast as you can to protect yourself and your family. The wild humans do the same thing. They know what's in your heart and if they see you as a threat, they'll leave or chase you away. If they have young, they'll chase you away. If one is ill and is having a problem, they'll chase you away.

They won't leave one behind that is hurt or sick. They'll stay and protect their family member. They look out for their own.

I believe without a doubt that if you hurt or kill one and he is not alone, the others will attack you and kill your sorry ass. You would deserve everything that they would do to you. And, yes, I would be on their side. They are a noble tribe and deserve respect.

I've learned a lot about myself and was forced to look deep inside myself at the kind of man I was. In the time I've spent with him, I've grown and have gained a knowledge that can't be learned in books. They are a lot like the Native Americans before the white fools came and killed them for their land. They lived off the land and only took what was needed to live and were thankful for the things that the earth had given them. They had a great love and respect for all things that shared the earth with them. They were a noble people and I hold them with the highest respect... we could have learned so much about our world. But, as stupid white men, we chose to take what was not ours and destroy it. We will do the same thing to the wild humans. We'll find them and kill them or put them in cages - all in the name of science and money.

When there are only two left, only then will we decide they are worth saving. But it'll be too late.

    I sat back in my chair, stunned. Mike likely had no idea the gift he had just given me. Every account, every sentence, every detail - if true - was more information than

I'd gleaned in all my years of research. I stared at nothing for a long time, processing everything I'd just read.

Was it true?

My gut told me it was.

My mind, of course, still reserved judgment - and I allowed for that. It's imperative, especially with anecdotal evidence, not to lose one's objectivity. However, despite the rather sensational subject matter, I had no reason to doubt Mike's story, simply because he had given me none. When I stepped back, objectively, and looked at the big picture: the details of his encounters, his overall observations of the creature's appearance and behavior, what I'd learned about Mike as a person, the way he had related information a bit at a time at first... and how now, having read all of this, I could find no contradictions.

-11-

SKUNK APE POO

During the last half of October, our phone calls continued, more frequently now. We were in a delicate spot in our relationship: I could tell that Mike, having shared so many intimate details of his encounters with me, was having mixed feelings. I was brimming with questions, but I was careful not to overload him. I posed questions tentatively - and he answered just as tentatively. Mostly, I just continued to listen, and let Mike talk.

When we first began talking in September, he had briefly mentioned that he would be returning to his camp over the Thanksgiving weekend. We'd had a couple of conversations early on about proof and protection, about Mike taking a camera to the swamp, trying to obtain physical evidence and documenting the collection of it on video. Now, he reiterated his plan to head up there at the end of November, and we started to discuss the logistical side of things. He expressed the need to get a camera - the only one he had was damaged in a fire long before.

"Can you point me in the right direction?" he asked. "What kind should I get?"

After some thought, I decided to point him towards the Sony Handy cams. I had an old TRV-310 that I'd paid an arm and a leg for a decade ago that still worked great, and I still used it regularly in the field. It had Nightshot - a setting that would turn on an infrared lamp and allow the user to "see" in the dark. Images shot in Nightshot appear slightly grainy and tinted green, but it would address Mike's concern of low light even in the daytime under the thick canopy in the swamp. I told Mike he could pick one up used for about $200 on EBay. Since I didn't know his financial situation, and didn't feel comfortable asking, I figured it was a good choice all the way around.

"What would you need," Mike asked, "in order to prove it without a body?"

We had come back around to our first conversation. I answered slowly, revisiting all of the times I'd thought about this. "DNA, I suppose. If you could get him to lick a plate clean, the saliva would be testable. But I would think the plate would need to be washed first with bleach, handled with gloves both when you put it out and collect it... put into a bag and sealed... if you could film him licking the plate and you collecting it, the video evidence would go a long way toward supporting test results if they came back 'unknown primate'..."

I thought some more. "Hair would be helpful, in addition to the saliva. If you could collect some hair... would he let you brush him?"

Mike snorted. I took that as a 'no'. "What about fly strips?" I asked. "Could you wrap a piece of fruit in a fly strip and toss it to him? It would probably pick up hair from him if he handled it..."

"I could just toss the fly strip at him," Mike said. I tried to visualize that and didn't know what to say. "Um... that could work..." I answered. I mentioned dandruff and scabs again...

I did my best to answer his question, but I didn't push... although I had some ideas, I wasn't sure exactly what we'd do with the evidence if he did obtain it. I knew it would need to be tested - independently, by a lab that was unbiased and perhaps didn't know *why* they were testing it. Good video evidence would go a long way toward backing up any "unknown" results. The question of what to do with 'unknown' lab results and good video evidence was even more intimidating. Bring a panel of scientists together? Have them sign non-disclosure agreements before the fact? How would *that* work? Ask them to write their papers, propose taxonomy, have the video analyzed and somehow take all of it to the legislature and try to get a law passed before the public found out and it was open hunting season on the Big Guys?

I figured, though, that it might be a good idea for him to try to get what he could while he had the opportunity; if it was in hand, we could ultimately worry about how to specifically deal with it after the fact.

"It would be ideal if you could get clear images of his feet, hands and face," I said. "Photos or casts of tracks would help, too." The feet, I thought, were especially important. Dr. Jeff Meldrum, Associate Professor of Anthropology at Idaho State University, had a collection of over 200 track casts. If he could examine tracks - as well as images of the feet that had made them - it would provide further corroboration of a huge body of evidence - the track casts - that had already been amassed and studied at length by a proponent in the academic world.

"If you could set up another camera that would film *you* filming *him*," I said, "that would help, too." I knew that it would quiet the critics who might cry 'Hoax!' when viewing first-person film evidence. "Here's how you do it, in a nutshell," I said. "You set up a camera at the edge of the camp to film the entire scene. Get him set up with the plate, toss him the fly strip, whatever. Then, you hold the other camera in your lap, maybe under a jacket or something, and film him..."

Even as I said it, it sounded ridiculous. But it was the best I could come up with. It reminded me of all of the emails I'd gotten over the years from guys saying, "It's easy... just grab a tranquilizer gun, get in a helicopter..." Great in theory - not so practical in application.

I didn't hold out much hope. It wasn't that I didn't believe that Mike's contact with the creature was close enough to obtain the evidence. I was simply trying to picture Mike, sitting in the swamp, doing all of these weird things and the Skunk Ape sitting there and taking it without raising an eyebrow. It just didn't seem feasible. This wasn't an inanimate object Mike would be interacting with. It was a big, wild creature - and presumably dangerous if pissed off.

This made me consider something else. "About the infrared..." I said to Mike.

"What about it?" he asked.

"There's some indication that they may be able to see it. Use it carefully and sparingly, if you do get an infrared camera." I sent Mike a couple of links to used Sony cameras on EBay.

A couple of days later, I got an email from him.

I need to take a little pause... I will be in touch when I can.

I had a feeling Mike was a little overwhelmed. While I'd done everything I could to sit back and simply let him direct our conversations, I knew that none of this could be easy for him. He was finally spilling the beans about something he'd experienced for a long time but had never told anyone about, and now we were discussing taking it even further. I was fine with giving him the space he needed.

* * * * *

We were out of touch for about a week. In the meantime, a friend of mine, a researcher in Texas, called me. We were talking about a lead I'd given him that he'd been following up on, and somehow he ended up doing a George Bush impersonation in the course of the conversation. I was amazed at how accurate it was. "Wouldn't it be funny," I asked, "if ol' W. was a Bigfoot researcher, interviewing Elvis as a witness? I wonder what that would sound like."

I soon found out. He sent me a clip of him, as George W., interviewing Elvis. The impersonations were dead on. I was amused... and posted it on YouTube and the blog.

Bigfoot research can be a serious and frustrating endeavor... and sometimes, a grin helps me bear it. The clip was a dead-on vocal impersonation of George W. - as the investigator - interviewing Elvis, who'd sighted a Sasquatch on his porch, found footprints "all around his Caddy", and was "all shook up". In the clip, my friend made a veiled reference to Dick Cheney and the quail hunting episode, in which Cheney accidentally shot a man with birdshot, saying (as George W.): "I got a guy... heh heh... he's pretty good with a gun. Worked with him a long time. Gonna send him out there... see if he can scare up what this is..." I was so busy being amazed by my friend's ability to impersonate these characters so accurately that the gun reference didn't even register.

I heard from Mike shortly after that.

Maybe you and that ass clown think it's funny to joke about sending someone out with a gun to find Bigfoot. But I don't think it's funny at all. It's one thing to carry a gun to protect yourself and another to carry one to kill a Bigfoot. ... I made a mistake contacting you. I think you're a good person but you are too close to the ones I want to protect him from. I am sorry it worked out like this but too much is at stake and I don't know who to trust. And speaking of trust: how can I trust someone who makes jokes about killing a Bigfoot and posts crap like that? I can't afford to take any chances with my friend's life. I owe him that much. I will send you a photo of him, and maybe when you look into his eyes you will see what I see and understand why I feel the way I do. Other than that, I won't be in contact with you anymore. Thanks for listening. It was great talking to you.

Like we say in the swamp... smell ya

Mike and the Big Guy

I felt dazed by Mike's email. I hadn't even considered the implications of the humor. I tried to call him, but he didn't answer.

I emailed him back:

I left you a message this morning, but I feel the need to write. I'm feeling pretty upset right now.

I never realized, not for a moment, that his humor would be taken like this. The reference he made to "a guy with a gun" was a veiled reference to Dick Cheney and the hunting incident (from the perspective of George Bush. It was big news and fodder for a lot of political humor during Bush's presidency). I got the joke as soon as he said it - the joke being about Dick Cheney and the running joke that the vice president went around shooting people - not about seriously killing or injuring a Sasquatch.

It never dawned on me that anyone would think for one moment that I would condone hurting one of these creatures in any way - everyone who knows me knows where I stand on that. Looking at it, I suppose the humor could be misconstrued, and I'm horrified to think that anyone would think that I would feel that way. I've placed a note on the YouTube video to that effect.

[This investigator] is one of the sweetest people I know and is not interested in shooting a Bigfoot anymore than I am. It was political humor... he was doing impressions for me on the phone one day, and I asked him what it would sound like if George Bush, as a Bigfoot investigator, interviewed Elvis, as an eyewitness. That was his take on it.

I understand that you are protective of your guy. SO AM I. I've spent two decades doing everything I can to understand and protect them and I don't know what more I can possibly do to make you understand that. It hurts me to think that someone, anyone, would think so poorly of me and my intentions when they are, and have always been, nothing but the best when it comes to the safety of the Big Guys.

I'm sorry you misunderstood. It wasn't intended to offend anyone or condone anything destructive - he was just being the silly guy I've always known.

Autumn

>Mike wrote back:

Ok, I get it and it still ain't funny... You need to understand that I come from a different world than you. There ain't no bunny rabbits and butterflies where I come from. I am not mad at you... after all, you are only human, and I should not hold you up to Big Guy standards. If you want to know where I am coming from, click on our document. I gave you a short look into my life. You will more than likely run screaming into the woods or something like that after you read it and I would not blame you if you did. You will see why it's hard for me to trust people...

    I clicked on the document, and read. And understood.
    Mike had written several pages about his life and the things he'd experienced in his past. Suddenly, the reasons for his desire to escape the world and head for the swamp were crystal clear: this man had endured more tragedy, through no fault of his own, than anyone had a right to. I suddenly not only understood his inability to trust, I could see why his relationship with the Big Guy meant so much to him. He'd been on the brink of hell - and his friend had helped bring him back.
    I realized at that point that my relationship with Mike - distrusting, grouchy, big-hearted Mike - was not so different from his relationship with the Big Guy. The balance was delicate, misunderstandings were bound to occur when you were dealing with an enigma wrapped in a mystery, and all you could do was your very best to allow the other to remain in control.
    I wrote him back:

I read what you posted on there and I hurt for you.

The irony to me here is that my friendship with you is not so different from your friendship with him. It amounts to pretty much the same thing - befriending and caring about someone who doesn't trust easily. But you've made mistakes just as I have... otherwise, you wouldn't have been thrown in the creek for poking him with a stick, right? The difference is, he didn't get up and walk away for good, leaving you sitting there with a bewildered look on your face, all of the time you'd spent caring about him and trying to understand him amounting to nothing.

I am a researcher second. A friend first. That's how I feel about you, and that's how I feel about the Big Guys. Always have, always will.

Again, ironically, if you were to sit down with him and have a conversation, I suspect it would go something like the one I'm about to have with you.

There are people in this world you can trust, and people you cannot. People, even those you CAN trust, will rarely behave "perfectly" in your eyes, probably because you come from a place that is difficult for them to understand. But who you put your trust in, ultimately, will determine your fate because, like it or not, we all coexist on this planet and you're bound to interact with others at some point. There are people who WILL genuinely reach out to you, who DO care. Those are the ones who deserve your patience, because there are rewards for trusting people - like genuine friendship and being on the receiving end of real affection. Snapperhead.

Autumn

Mike replied with his typical humor:

I was thinking about you all day and feeling like crap. Felt like I broke up with my best girlfriend: not the one with the hairy legs and the tattoo... the other one with the dirty neck and stringy hair.

I feel bad for showing my ass... you don't deserve to be treated like that and, yes, I am a Snapperhead. I think I was more pissed at him than at you - I do not like Bigfoot researchers and never will and when I hear Bigfoot and guns in the same sentence, I want to go Skunk Ape on someone's ass.

I don't want you to hurt for me - that ain't why I told you that stuff. I just wanted you to know what you were dealing with so that you might understand why I do some of the things I do. And why I feel the way I do about things and why I don't trust people and almost never give second chances. As far as the Big Guy goes, I know what I am going to do and it protects him and me and lets people get to know him. And when the people get to know him they will love him and demand that he be protected. It's not a great plan but it's the only one that I have so I will go with it.

Mike

P.S. I wrote this song just for you. It goes to the Joe Stampley song "Do You Ever Fool Around"...

What do you get a girl who has everything?
Do you get her diamonds and fancy things?
Let me tell you what I do...
I always get her Skunk Ape poo
Yes, I get her Skunk Ape poo
I bag it up just for you

And when your friends ask, 'What did you get?"
Smile and say, "A bag of Skunk Ape shit!"
Yes, I give her Skunk Ape poo
Only the best will do for you...

...It ain't done yet.

   I wrote back:

You crack me up, Snapperhead.

Just let me know if there's anything I can do to help you. With anything, I mean, not just the Big Guy. I'm happy to be a sounding board, or whatever.

That's what friends do.

And I'd rather NOT receive any Skunk Ape poo, if it's all the same to you. We'll just say it's the thought that counts.

   We'd gotten through it. Somehow. Because that's what friends do.

–12–

RETURN TO THE SWAMP

"I call him Enoch," Mike told me.

"Why?" I asked.

"Because of this sound he makes all the time. 'E-knock. E-knock'," Mike mimicked in a guttural voice.

* * * * *

Mike was getting serious. He had gone out and purchased six game cameras and was following leads on used Sony Handycams in his area. The second weekend in November rolled around, and he made a preliminary journey to the swamp.

I got an email from him on Sunday, November 15th.

There is another river where I'd seen tracks and I followed them for about twenty miles north. I got the cameras to see if there were any more coming up or down river. I set the cameras up and am going to leave them there until I come back the following week.

Swamp flooded... camp has a foot of water in it. Lots of snakes... it ain't looking good. If the water don't go down soon, he won't come around. I'm going to look for him in the pine woods. There is this place he likes to go. I think he's around because deer stands are being torn down in that area. If he is there, he'll find me. I'm looking for signs now with no luck... everything is underwater. I guess that's why they call it a swamp.

I'm driving my boat where we used to walk. That storm really dumped a lot of water last week.

Just thought I would give you an update. I can't call ya... I have a bad infection in both my ears and I can't hear nothing. Doc said I waited to long to see her and it's really bad and will take a while to clear up. I shouldn't be out here today but I needed to check on things and needed to get away.

I'm floating down this river writing you this, trying to see how long I can keep a signal on my air card... three bars and fading. You wouldn't like it here today - lots of snakes in the trees and water.

I am coming back up on the 25th. Maybe things will be better by then and maybe I will be able to hear something. Right now, I can't hear anything. I can hardly hear the motor running. Never had it this bad before. Got to head back around noon - it's a long drive and I don't feel so good today and want to get back and get some sleep.

Smell ya later, Autumn Gator...

MIKE

Surreal. It's the only way to describe how I felt about getting an email from Mike, who was floating down a river next to the swamp, telling me in real time about his journey. *Technology is amazing,* I thought. But more than that: it really outlined the difference between the "wilderness" in Florida and that of Oregon, and how humans had encroached upon the Big Guys there. If I were out in Bigfoot's backyard in my home state, there wouldn't be a wireless signal for miles.

Mike wrote me again a couple of days later, when he was back in civilization:

I took my laptop into the swamp to see if I could get a signal. It don't work in the swamp but it does on the river. I'm trying to find out how to send you a live cam shot of the Big Guy. I could do it from the sand bar but it would have to be at night so nobody would see us and I don't know how that would work.

My big plan was to have a live internet hookup that people could log onto and see the Big Guy live for as long as he will sit still. I think that would be better than telling people where he is, and people could see what I see live. Think about how many people would see it world wide… Do you think that would be proof enough for them? I have my geek working on it to see how it can be done. I'll have to spend a lot of money, but if it works, it'll be worth it. What do you think would happen if I were able to pull it off?

Keep checking docs… I may tell you the rest of the story sometime. I still feel funny talking about it. I have the whole story written down in another file but I'm afraid to show you… Maybe after you meet the Big Guy and I have proof to back it up.

Smell ya later, Autumn Gator

A week passed, as Mike prepared for his trip. He managed to track down and purchase a used Sony Handycam. I thought a lot about what might happen over the long Thanksgiving weekend.

The funny thing was, I really didn't feel like *I* needed proof. I was willing to support Mike in his desire to attempt to prove their existence and do everything I could to help figure out if we could use that evidence to help protect them. I would have loved to see a photograph, if only to reconcile the image that was burned into my mind as a child, to gaze upon that wild visage with an adult's eye and validate what I remembered seeing. But the more we talked about it, the less sure I was that proof would provide protection for these creatures. It seemed to me that Mike had his hand on the lid of Pandora's Box.

What I didn't really understand was that Mike was determined to prove it to *me*.

I knew Mike was leaving on Wednesday afternoon after work. I didn't expect to hear from him until the following week. But then I remembered that he could stay in contact off and on while he was out there, as long as he went out to the river. I checked our online document. Sure enough... he had written. I had no idea he was planning to keep a running journal.

On the precipice of a five-day weekend, Mike entered the swamp again... and, for the first time, he had an agenda.

Wednesday 11/25/2009

Left work at 3:00 p.m. Boat hooked to truck, loaded and ready to go, it's raining and I have a long drive ahead of me.

Got to the boat ramp at 10:00 p.m. ... running late, had to stop by [the other river] and get the six camera traps I set out a week ago. Nothing on them but deer, one bear, coons, kids on four wheelers, hunters... no Big Guys or Big Girls.

Floated boat, parked truck, walking back, cop pulls up, we talk for a while.

Cop left, I fired up the engine and headed out into the darkness. Headed downriver as fast as I could go, could not wait to get to camp.

Pulled into the creek - it was dark and spooky, just the way I remember it. Pulled up to camp. The place was a mess - water has gone down but everything is wet and muddy. Too nasty to use right now. I'll have to come back later when it dries and clean up and run off the snakes and gators.

Went back to the old camp on the sandbar under the big oak tree. It's dry there - no mud, only sand. Walked around, looking for tracks and found none, but I know he is here. I can feel it.

The moon is up and I can see ok, but it's too late to make camp tonight. I've been up since 4:00 a.m. and worked all day, then drove here, and I'm beat. Going to sleep on the boat tonight and set up camp tomorrow.

It's a little past midnight. Maybe he will come around later when he finds out I'm here. I'm worried he won't show. I've got a lot riding on this - it's put up or shut up time, and I need to get some shots of him for Autumn.

I got six camera traps, a Sony nightshot camcorder, Bionic Ear sound amplifier, digital recorder and a lot of Hershey bars and Blue Birds. And one secret weapon that I can't talk about because it's a secret.

Mike stayed at the river camp on the sandbar, making forays into the swamp.

Thursday 11/26/2009

It's Turkey day; sitting here eating some eggs and bacon. It's really a nice day. Thank you, Lord, for making it for me.

I got up early and walked out into the swamp, looking around. It's still got a lot of water in it - could not go far. I will set up the cameras around camp and go looking for him upriver in the pine woods.

7:00 p.m.: Looked all over the pine woods today... Nothing, no signs at all, not looking good. It's just a waiting game for now. Maybe I will have better luck tomorrow. Lots of hunters around - they could have made him go deeper into the swamp. Autumn called me around 1:00 p.m. to wish me a Happy Thanksgiving... It was nice to hear from her. It really made my day even better. Too bad she ain't here - I think she would get a kick out of this trip. I think the world of her and would like to show her some of my world and let her meet the Big Guy.

I got all the cameras on and I am ready for the Big Guy to show himself. Got all his favorite foods. It will be good to see him again. It's been much too long.

It's cold here tonight. Got plenty of firewood, so it won't be too bad. I am the only one around for miles. All the other camps are empty. This weekend they will all be full of people hunting and fishing, but for now, I have it all to myself.

So I'm sitting by the fire writing this, wondering if I'm going to look up and see him standing there. I hope he shows up soon. It's lonely here tonight and I'm starting to feel it. Got a big steak cooking on the fire... smells good... also got a tater wrapped in foil along with some corn on the cob, some sweet cold slaw and a jug of sweet tea. I do eat good when I'm in the woods. I just don't like eating alone. Maybe a coon will come by for some leftovers and we can chat awhile.

Steak's done... gotta go.

10:30 p.m.: Going downriver [several] miles to check a few spots where he might be - some of his old stomping grounds. I'm starting to get a weird feeling like something is out there - a feeling like I'm being watched. I feel something is out there, and I don't think it's him. I'm going to leave for a few hours and see if it comes into camp when I am gone. The feeling is so strong that I feel the need to wear my gun... He ain't the only thing that lives out here and walks around in the dark.

The whole place has a different feel to it, like something has changed, and not in a good way.

Friday 11/27/2009

Went downriver last night, looking for the Big Guy. Found some tracks on the river bank. He is heading toward camp. I'm sure I drove past him in the dark. And he has a friend with him - the second set of tracks are smaller, maybe his mate. That would be cool.

It's cold here and I didn't get much sleep. Something is out there in the woods moving around but I can't see nothing. I only hear sticks breaking as it moves around. I'll look for tracks and try to find out what it is... maybe a new Big Guy is checking me out. Nothing on cameras last night. I had hopes that whatever it is would come into camp and I could get a photo.

Talked to some hunters last night downriver... they are camping at the place where the old hermit used to live. They told me that something has been following them around and that they hear strange sounds all the time. They said it was a Skunk Ape and this ain't the first time they had a run in with one out here. They said that there is a bunch of them living here and that they see them once in a while, but only from far off... nothing close up. I didn't tell them that I already knew that or what I was doing out there. They think I'm hunting.

Forty degrees don't sound cold to people who live in the snow, but down here, it's like being in a deep freezer. The wind makes it cut you to the bone. But it warms up fast once the sun comes up. By noon, I'll be wearing just a shirt.

Those tracks are heading this way. I think I'll see him today. I got a good feeling about it... am going to hang close to camp and wait, maybe do some fishing. Some fried catfish would be good. I'm sitting here thinking what culinary delight I'm going to make for breakfast. Maybe some smoked sausage and hot cakes with cane syrup.

Had the best dream last night. It's been a while... It must be where I am. I can feel the stress melting away, making a big puddle at my feet. I'm feeling alive again. The sun is warming my bones and as I look around at the river, I get a peaceful easy feeling come over me. That must be what the Eagles were singing about. I wish I could stay here forever. What a great day this is...

what a great day. I am standing on the edge of a great day and I feel good.

3:30 p.m.: Went fishing most of the day and rode up to the boat ramp to check on my pickup. The river has come alive with people going fishing and hunting, the camps along the river are filling up fast. It's going to be a wild weekend on the old river - all I can do is try to stay out of the way. I hope they don't scare the Big Guy away.

Still no sign of him in camp... those tracks might not have been his, or maybe he's too busy with his sweetheart. I don't know what else I can do but wait; if he don't show up soon I guess I will have to wait some more.

Walked in the woods around [the river] camp looking for signs of what has been moving around. I see some big depressions in the leaves, broken limbs, and a trail in a half moon where it circles the camp. It must walk back and forth trying to see me. Also, there is a big area that looks like it sat or laid down. I took some food, hung it on a tree about seven feet off the ground, and pointed a camera at it... maybe I will get a shot of it tonight.

It could be a bear, but a bear would have come into camp when I left last night. And if it's the Big Guy, he would've let me know that he was there. But still I don't like being watched... if it comes back tonight, I am going get my Q-Beam out of the boat and light his ass up.

7:00 p.m.: Just got done with supper and I am going to go downriver to look for the Big Guy. I've got to find him... I am running out of time. If he was here, he would have showed himself by now. I wonder if he forgot about me or lost interest in me or found something else to keep him busy. I'm sure those were tracks I saw last night... it's hard to tell in the sugar sand - they just look like big holes in the sand with no detail to them.

I called Autumn and she thinks I should take down the cameras and get back to the way it was before. I think I'll go over to the creek camp and hang out there tonight and see if that makes a difference. My phone and laptop won't work in there so I'll be out of touch for a while.

Mike had called me from the river camp. He told me how things were going... or rather, that they weren't. When he told me that he had six camera traps up on the trees, I groaned. "Well, no *wonder* nothing's happening! Hurry... go take them down!" I told him. I had no idea that he was planning to plaster the woods with camera traps.

I had pictured Mike visiting with the creature, getting comfortable again, introducing any cameras slowly, testing the waters, and maybe putting one on the second or third day after he'd made contact again... I told him so. "Imagine that you've lived in the same house for 30 years," I said. "Then you come home one day, walk through the front door, and someone has put a new painting on the wall. How long do you think it will take you to notice it? I guarantee you he's avoiding the area because of those cameras."

Mike answered, "Okay, okay. I'll go take 'em down."

He told me he was going to the creek camp that night. I hoped, for his sake, that the cameras hadn't ruined the trust he'd spent so long building. I wished him luck, and we hung up.

The next time I talked to Mike, it sounded like he was lucky to be alive.

-13-

FEELING WATCHED

Saturday 11/28/2009

I'm back. It's 9:30 p.m. on Saturday night, 11/28/2009. Couldn't post anything last night. Went to creek camp. Here's what happened:

After talking to Autumn, I took down all the camera traps and put them away. Then I got some food and firewood and went over to the creek camp. After building a fire, I sat down and waited to see if the Big Guy would show up.

Around 11:00 p.m., I heard a whoop and a whistle. I looked up and saw him peeking around a tree at the edge of camp. At first, he didn't want to come in. He just stood behind that tree, making a chattering sound. I said, "Come on, I got some food for you," holding out some fruit. Still nothing, so I went to him. It was one of the few times he let me walk up to him... I knew something was wrong.

I held out a bag of apples and he reached around the tree, took them, and walked into the darkness. I went back and sat down, not sure what was going on. A short time later, he came back, walking into camp, like he was afraid. He was looking around like he lost something. I think he was looking for the cameras, but they were in the boat in a box where he couldn't see them.

I went to the boat and got a box of fruit and bread for him. He took it and sat down on the log and started to eat. He was chattering like a monkey, talking up a storm. I've never seen him act like this before, and it had me worried.

He took the loaf of bread and looked at it and then at me, then back at the bread. Something was wrong with the bread. Looking at it I said, "Oh, crap... I forgot the honey." I went to the boat, got a jar of honey and poured some on the bread. He loves that. I went back to the boat and put the honey back in the food locker.

While I was there, I got the camcorder, turned it on, and was fooling around with it, pointing it everywhere but at him. He was watching me and he didn't seem to mind, so I slowly pointed it at him and started filming him eating. He stopped for a second, and then went back to eating.

I turned back toward the boat, turned on the nightshot, and did the same thing, slowly walking around camp. I turned toward him, pointed it at his feet and slowly moved upward. I was about eight feet in front of him and moved it up to his face.

BIG MISTAKE.

In one quick move, he lunged at me, holding his hand out, fingers spread wide. I had no time to react - it happened in a split second: he grabbed the camera, shoving it hard into my chest. I went flying backward through the air, landing headfirst in the boat. He took the camera and crushed it with one hand... then, slamming it to the ground, he let out a scream and ran into the swamp.

I lay there for a while, not able to move. I was in a lot of pain and stuck, wedged in headfirst on my left side. I finally got up and sat down on the seat and I could see blood everywhere. My shirt was soaked red, my head hurt; my left arm was scraped bad up to my shoulder. I touched the left side of my head above my ear. It was bloody and hurt to the touch and I could feel the blood running down my neck.

I tried to get out of the boat and slipped and fell onto the ground. I got up on my knees and had to hold onto the boat to steady myself. I felt dizzy and weak and like I was going to throw up... and then did. I sat beside the boat, resting my head on the gunnel and passed out.

When I woke up, the fire had almost gone out and the sun was coming up. I was cold and weak. I crawled over to the camera and picked it up... it was mashed. I knew how it felt.

Crawling back to the boat, I got in and went back to the river camp.

I ran the bow up on the sand, got out and stumbled into camp. I felt weak and dizzy and climbed into my sleeping bag, pulling another one over me. I went to sleep and slept 'til late in the afternoon.

Around 4:30 p.m., I heard something walking around camp. Slowly taking my pistol out of the holster, I eased the cover off my head and took a look around and there he was standing with his back to me. Still lying down, I pointed it at him and cocked the hammer back. He turned and froze, staring at the gun now pointed at his head, my finger on the trigger. I was still covered with blood from the night before. I said to him, "Get your sorry ass out of here, you son of a bitch, before I forget that we're friends." He turned and ran into the woods. I rolled over and went back to sleep and when I awoke it was dark.

Getting up, I started a fire and took off my shirt, heated up some water, and washed the dried blood off me. I got my first aid kit and patched myself up as best I could... and after looking in the mirror, I can add a black eye to my list. Ate some soup and crackers and I feel better now.

It's cold and I want to go home. I have had enough of this crap. I will stay tonight and pack up and go home in the morning. If that asshole comes around me tonight, I'm going to go Skunk Ape on his ass. It's 11:40 p.m. now and no sign of him. Don't feel like sleeping... think I will just set here by the fire for a while.

Ain't heard from Autumn... I guess she has better things to do than fool with my dumb ass. What's the point in doing any of this crap anyway? It don't matter what I do... at the end of the day, I'm still in this alone, getting my ass beat for nothing. I'm sitting here bloody and beaten, cold and alone, wishing I had a bottle of fuck-it-all. I know more about this than all them stupid ass-wipes. They would've crapped themselves if they'd have been here last night. And I know if they were here last night they would not be here now, bunch of sissy ass-clowns.

And they call themselves "experts"... what a bunch of losers. If they know so much, how come none of them have a Skunk Ape to kick their ass? But some people think dumb assholes like them do good work. Don't quit your day job. That's right... you jackass, numb-nutted, tree-knocking turd spots.

Well, I feel better now... venting is a lot of fun, don't you think? Oh, well... I am going to take a boat ride. No... I am going to bed. It's 1:40 a.m., Sunday.

Sunday 11/29/2009

8:20 a.m.: The most amazing thing happened last night. It has me shook up and excited and I am trying to understand what happened.

I was sleeping and felt something kick my foot. I thought I was dreaming, so I rolled over, pulling the blanket over my head. It kicked me again... This time, I knew it was not a dream and did not move. It kicked me again. I rolled over, looking up and it was my friend, the big hairy mud-sucker that beat my ass for pointing a camera at him.

I sat up and said, "What do you want? Did you come back to kick my ass again, or are you hungry? Well, whatever the reason, I'm sore and I don't feel well and my head hurts, thank you very much. You know where the food is... help yourself. I'm going back to sleep." I lay back down, pulling the blanket over my head. He reached down, pulled the blanket off me, and stepped back, dropping the blanket to the ground. "Hey, Snapperhead, it's cold! Give me that back! I don't feel like doing this right now. Did I not say that I didn't feel well? Now leave me alone." He just stood there next to the big oak and stared at me.

Getting up and grabbing my coat, I tossed some wood on the fire. I walked over to him, looked him right in the eye and said, "Ok... I'm up. Now what is it? What do you want?" He didn't move. He just stared into my eyes, so I stared back waiting to see what he was going to do.

I started to feel strange and took a step back, not taking my eyes off his. Then it happened... it came rushing over me: a feeling of deep sadness and despair. It felt like I was swimming in sadness. It was taking over me and I started to shake. My legs felt like rubber; I thought I was going to fall down. My eyes started to water and I felt like was going to cry. The feeling was so overwhelming that I couldn't stop it. I looked at him. Tears were running down his face - his eyes were watering. It was not me that was sad - it was him.

I was feeling what he was feeling. It was overpowering. I had the feeling of deep sorrow and a wanting to be forgiven. I said to him, "I know you didn't mean to hurt me. I'm not mad at you... I was wrong for doing what I did. I'm sorry and want you to forgive me. Hell, you are my only friend and you're allowed to kick my ass once in awhile. I'm truly sorry. I will never do it again and to show you I mean what I say, come with me..." I walked down to the boat, wiping the tears from my eyes. He followed me, stopping about halfway there.

I reached into the boat and pulled out the box that I had the cameras in. Opening the lid, I took two out and held them up so he could see. I said, "Never again will I try to hurt you with these," and threw them in the river. I got two more and threw them as far as I could into the river. Grabbing the last two, I did the same with them. I took the bionic ear and threw it in as well. I took the smashed Sony camcorder and walked over to him. He stepped back. I held it up to him and said, "Do you understand? Never again will I do this." I turned and threw it as far as I could. Then I turned and looked into his eyes. "Do you understand what I mean, Vern? Never again."

I walked past him, slapping him on the arm and said, "Are you hungry? Do ya wanna eat? Come on." As I walked back to camp, I could feel the sadness leave my body, pouring off me like water, leaving my soul clean and new.

He stood there for a while looking out into the river. The moon was bright and I could see the moonlight reflecting off the white sand, almost glowing around him. I stood there in awe, looking at what a magnificent creature he is, and thinking how lucky I am that he lets me into his world.

Sunday 11/29/2009

8:10 p.m.: I made it home and I am glad it's over with. I'm sore and can hardly move without hurting somewhere. It'll take me a while to get over this. I've been up since 3:00 a.m. when I got woke up. It's been a wild night and I have a lot to think about.

We sat in camp until sun-up and we came to an understanding, I think. I tried some of the things that Autumn told me to do - and in some weird way, I think she is onto something. I went Spock on him and did a mind meld, so to speak, and I think for the first time we really understood each other.

He ate and then leaned back against that big old oak and closed his eyes. I sat in my chair in front of him and stared at him and tried to see inside his head. After a while, he opened his eyes and looked into mine. We sat like that for two hours and in all that time he never moved - not so much as a blink of an eye. I saw things in my mind's eye and felt things that I don't understand, but in the end, I think I have a better understanding of what he is all about. I'll go into more detail some other time. I'm tired and need to get some sleep. I have to be at work at 6:00 a.m.

Monday 11/30/2009

Last night, I woke up three times with Big Guy on my mind and when I got up this morning, I had him on my mind. I couldn't stop thinking about him and the things that happened last weekend. The thoughts were so strong that I could hardly work. All I could think about was him. Then around 10:30 a.m., it came to me like a switch was turned on and I could see it all clearly... I understood what it meant. And why things went the way they did on the river.

The night of Thanksgiving, I got a bad feeling that something was watching me. I also had a strong feeling that I needed to protect myself. Not from him, but from something unknown. A feeling that something had changed - and in a bad way. I had a bad feeling about being there, like something was going to happen. I felt nervous and on edge and wanted to get out of there. It was like a distant fear of something unknown.

I've never been afraid like that before, even when I should have been. This was different: it was a fear and mistrust of something I couldn't see. And as I wrote it down on my laptop, the feeling got stronger. I could feel the eyes on me. I could feel them staring at me and I felt fear and I didn't understand why, until today.

It came to me so clearly that I could almost see it in my mind's eye.

It wasn't <u>me</u> who was afraid. It was <u>him</u>. He was the one who saw the eyes looking at him. He was the one not trusting what he didn't understand. He wanted to see me but was afraid I'd changed and wanted to hurt him in some way. He was the one wanting get away from there - not me. I was feeling what he was *feeling. It was almost like he was trying to let me know that he was afraid - afraid to show himself for fear of what might happen.*

And when I pointed the camera at him, all he saw was the eye shining in his face and was afraid that I was using the eye to hurt him. The end result was me getting the crap knocked out of me and scaring the only friend I have in the world who understands me.

Right after I got this understanding, I got a strong feeling that he was pleased and happy that I understood. I saw this as clear as daylight - it was like he was telling me why things went the way they did. Looking back, I can see that he tried to tell me Sunday morning when we sat under that old oak staring at each other. But my mind was not open to hear what he was saying. And he wanted me to know this: he was trying to warn me not to take his trust for granted. What he has given me he can take away and that would be a tragic loss for the both of us.

Autumn... I felt this in my soul. It was the most intense feelings I think I've ever had. What do you think?

    All day Sunday, I was running around like a chicken with my head cut off, being the single mom to a toddler. I didn't get a chance to sit down and check our online document again until Monday morning. After finally reading what had happened, I immediately called Mike. He answered, breaking his usual rule of not talking to me on the phone from work.
    Despite the fact that he had written it all down for me, he related again the events of Saturday night and Sunday to me over the phone in detail - the conversation lasted almost two hours. He was really shaken up by everything

that had happened and sounded terrible. When I asked him how he was feeling, he complained of being dizzy and lightheaded, that his head still hurt, and that he was pretty banged up. I urged him to go see a doctor; I was afraid he might have a concussion.

Mike repeatedly stressed to me how strong the feelings had been - the fear, the sense of "eyes" watching him, the intense sadness he experienced when Enoch returned on Sunday. I was intrigued by his description of this seemingly emotional, non-verbal communication between himself and the creature. I have come to know Mike as someone who is reluctant to interpret much of anything. He sticks to the facts and simply relays them in a matter-of-fact manner. Not only that: Mike simply isn't a "mushy" or "touchy-feely" kind of person. He's a man's man. His gruff exterior holds the world at arm's length and his personality doesn't lend itself to emotional displays. It was surprising to hear him emphasize, again and again, such powerful emotions. He was overwhelmed. I could hear it in his voice.

I knew how the story might sound to others - those who didn't know Mike like I did. I could hear the detractors now: *"How convenient. He threw the cameras in the river."* But I understood.

This man, who had gotten closer to one of these creatures than anyone I'd known, had become the very thing he hated: a "researcher" with an agenda. In his recounting of that night, I could hear the disgust in his voice. Despite the fact that he was ranting at me and everyone else in the world, I knew that he was very angry with *himself*.

It wasn't until almost two months later, when we were talking again about that weekend, that the full impact of it hit him.

"This has really been bothering me. When I called you from the river camp and you scolded me for putting those cameras up, I felt like an ass. As I took them down, I was feeling really disgusted with myself. I had become the one thing I hated most: a tree knocker. You didn't know how much your words stung me. But did I stop? No. Did I go all the way back to the way it was before? No. I'm ashamed to say that I didn't. I was hell-bent on getting a photo to prove to you that this was real. I felt like it was time to put-up or shut-up. So what did I do? I went out there and put that damned camera in his face and got my ass kicked for my troubles."

Even his established relationship with Enoch didn't save him from the creature's swift reaction to having a pointed at his face. (Enoch's reaction to the camera, once the infrared light was turned on, furthered my suspicion that these creatures can see infrared.)

"No more," I told him. "Don't do it again. I didn't require a picture to believe you in the first place, and it isn't worth your health or your safety."

"Don't worry about it," he replied, his voice dry with humor. "I don't have the camera anymore, anyway."

-14-

THE RENDEZVOUS

As our friendship continued to grow, so did Mike's willingness to share more of his encounters with me. I still wondered if it had something to do with the fact that I didn't require a picture or other "proof" to believe him. Throughout our telephone conversations, he began to, once again, tentatively allude to something in conversation - only to call or email me a couple of days later and tell me to "check the docs". When I did, there would be another explosion of information sitting there waiting for me to absorb.

"Remember," he said one day as we were well into another three-hour phone call, "when I mentioned something early on that there were others around?"

"Yeah," I said. I waited.

"Well... I was withholding stuff again. Sorry." He sounded hangdog. I laughed. Mike was always apologizing for not trusting me, for not telling me everything. And I was always telling him that he didn't need to apologize, that I understood, that he was welcome to share whatever he felt comfortable sharing. I learned a long time ago that respecting someone's boundaries, whatever they may be, is crucial to building a successful friendship, and I reminded him of that again.

"I know. I know. I just feel bad for not trusting you, not telling you everything. Anyway," he continued, "check the docs. I wrote something in there for you about that."

He went on to tell me most of the story over the phone. What he told me was astonishing - not simply due to what he had witnessed, but how, once again, Mike's experiences validated some of my own suspicions.

In August of 2006, I had published an article in my OregonBigfoot.com email newsletter about Bigfoot meeting places: specifically, breeding grounds. I was pregnant for the first time when I wrote it, and pregnancy was understandably on my mind. I began thinking about how Sasquatches might mate, and how a female would deal with the difficulty and inevitable vulnerability of pregnancy. Waddling around as I was, grossly uncomfortable in the comfort of my civilized, convenient world, I wondered how a pregnant Bigfoot would cope in the wild. Who would care for her, before and after the birth? Did infant Sasquatches cry at birth as human babies do? Was there a concern that someone might hear them?

That got me thinking: many long-term witnesses I'd interviewed had described noticing that the creatures seemed to vanish during certain times of the year, only to reappear during a change of season. The witness, Michelle whom I'd worked with in California had mentioned this. She also related that one year the creatures had returned in the spring and she'd watched a female, obviously pregnant before her disappearance, hold up an infant during a brief sighting, as if showing the witness her new offspring.

Then I considered the rare instances in which witnesses had reported seeing many creatures gathered in one location. I wondered if the two things might be related. Did Sasquatches did gather in groups larger than small family units? And if so, to what purpose? For breeding? For protection and care during late pregnancy and after birth? Or simply for communion with others of their kind? I decided to explore the idea and write an article about it for the newsletter.

Here is the full text of that article, as it was published in August of 2006:

Sasquatch Breeding Grounds?
By Autumn Williams

DOZENS OF SASQUATCH - ADULTS, JUVENILES AND INFANTS - COEXISTING IN A REMOTE BOX CANYON OVER THE WINTER...

Unfortunately, absolutely nothing is "known" about Sasquatch mating or breeding habits, since there's been no official discovery... and although eyewitnesses will tell you Bigfoot exists, the majority of the scientific community might argue otherwise. With that aside, I can offer some ideas I've been pondering about this for quite some time. This is the first time I've published anything in depth about this theory of mine... and let me remind you, it's only a theory. An idea. In no way do I attest that anything in this article is fact, only speculation. But if you'll humor me and read on, you may find this topic of speculation as fascinating as I do...

It's safe to say that Sasquatch would be a mammal - that is, a warm-blooded creature that is viviparous (gives birth to live offspring). Gestation, the period of time in which an embryo grows to a mature fetus within the womb, differs between mammal species. (I've learned a lot about this lately, being currently pregnant myself. *grin*) As a general rule, the larger *the mammal, the longer the gestation period. Human gestation takes approximately 266 days (an average of 9-10 months, depending whether you're counting from the date of conception or the LMP... last menstrual period.). African gorillas take somewhere in the neighborhood of 250 to 296 days, with an average of 8.5 months. Horses gestate for about 48 weeks, or 12 months. So gestation varies a lot, from species to species and within the individual pregnancy, depending on any number of factors.*

With those species as size comparisons though, let's take a stab at a Sasquatch gestation period. They're built similarly to a human, being bipedal, and although their upper torso may be similar in size to an adult gorilla's, there is extra leg mass to consider. On the low end, I'd guess 9 months. But due to the extra size of the creature, I'd venture to say that the gestation period might last 12 months - or longer.

Being pregnant myself, I have a new appreciation for how difficult life can be while you're carrying a child. And that's with all the "modern conveniences" we humans are used to... Sasquatch moms-to-be don't have the luxury of super markets, refrigerators, comfortable beds in warm homes... you get the idea.

While the question of whether Sasquatch is closer to human or animal is something still open to debate, (as are all things "Sasquatch"), I'd like to take this moment to make what may be a somewhat controversial suggestion:

I propose that Sasquatches may very well meet en masse in order to breed and give birth to young.

Now at first glance, this proposition may appear fanciful, too good to be true, even outrageous, but let me share my reasoning behind this idea... and where it came from.

There are a few stories of eyewitnesses claiming to observe family units and/or large gatherings of these creatures. Take, for instance, the story of Albert Ostman, who claimed a detailed encounter with a family group. Briefly, Ostman claimed to have been abducted near the Toba Inlet in British Columbia in 1924. After a harrowing night of being carried in his sleeping bag on the back of "something", he was finally set down and crawled out. He described interacting with a "family" of four creatures in a box canyon:

"I could see now that I was in a small valley or basin about eight or ten acres, surrounded by high mountains, on the southeast side there was a V-shaped opening about eight feet wide at the bottom and about twenty feet high at the highest point — that must be the way I came in." He also describes their shelter: "On my way back I noticed where these people were sleeping. On the east side wall of this valley was a shelf in the mountain side, with overhanging rock, looking something like a big undercut in a big tree about 10 feet deep and 30 feet wide."

When reading Ostman's account 16 years or so ago in John Green's book, <u>Sasquatch: The Apes Among Us</u>[1], I was certainly fascinated, but didn't give much thought at the time to family units and how they come to be. It wasn't until many years later that I revisited Ostman's story when an idea began brewing in my head.

---

[1] Read the full account, in Ostman's words: John Green, Sasquatch: The Apes Among Us (Surrey, BC: Hancock House Publishers. 2006), 99-110.

The next account I'd like to refer to is the story of Muchalat Harry, from 1928. Once again, it is the story of a man who was abducted while sleeping. This witness described a similar shelter to the one Albert Ostman described... however, the number of creatures he described was astounding: "When daylight came he was able to see that he was in a sort of camp, under a high rock shelf and surrounded by some twenty Bigfoot. They were of all sexes and sizes."[1]

The final story, and the one that ultimately caused me to examine Sasquatch breeding habits and the possibility that breeding and birthing may be a "community" phenomenon, was published in Seattle Magazine in August of 1970. It isn't widely disseminated; I found it quite by accident on the internet years ago. It's unclear whether the "Vancouver" referred to in this article is Vancouver, B.C. or Vancouver, WA. Since the paragraph precluding this one discussed the Ostman story within this same news article, I'm inclined to think it refers, once again, to the Vancouver, B.C. area.

"A similar story comes from Warren Scott, a 37-year-old Seattle man who works as a building superintendent. It was June of 1961, and Scott, who grew up in a tough neighborhood in New York City and spent several years bumming around after his release from the Army, was camping alone, 30 miles northeast of Vancouver. Late at night, a Sasquatch kidnapped him and carried him 70 miles. During the journey, Scott was almost suffocated by the creature's vice-like grip and uremic odor. Eventually, he was carried through a long tunnel and dumped in a cave.

---

[1] Read the full account: Peter Byrne, The Search for Bigfoot: Monster, Myth or Man? (New York: Pocket Books, 1976), 1-4.

"Most of Scott's ordeal was spent in this hot, fire-lit enclosure. The mother took care of him, bringing him food (greens and inedible chunks of raw meat); the old man was seldom around. 'I was treated like a pet,' Scott recalls.

"He endured some good-natured whacking on the rump; he was watched intently when passing wastes, and he engaged in some rock-rolling with the kids. The noise and the smell were terrific. At night, father, mother and son Sasquatch would hold each other tightly, rock for 10 minutes, and then drop off to sleep on bough beds.

"One day, Scott wandered out of the momentarily unguarded cave and was terrified to see 50 or 60 Sasquatch wandering about in the canyon. 'The female who fed me came up to me, grabbed me and held me to her bosom until I was calm. Then she put me down." Soon thereafter, Scott's protector took him, together with her own son, on a tour of the other caves, one of which proved to be a very busy nursery.

"A few days later, Scott located the densely curtained tunnel opening and made his escape."

What interested me about these three reports were the startling similarities between them. All three presumably occurred In British Columbia, contained an abduction of a human to a remote area (a hidden or box canyon) where multiple creatures were seen using caves or overhangs as shelters - and two of the reports contained elements of "tribal" Bigfoot gatherings.

Who knows whether ANY of these reports turn out to be true and accurate... but, for the sake of argument, let's assume there is truth to them. The final report, despite the strangeness of the *"fire-lit enclosure", really got me thinking. Scott claimed to have viewed a "nursery". Was this an isolated case? Perhaps. But Muchalat Harry described seeing multiple juvenile creatures as well.*

What would cause so many creatures to collect in such a small area? Wouldn't that number of bodies put an incredible strain on available food resources? Probably. But consider this...

Perhaps gathering for breeding and birthing would be beneficial.

Let's examine the following scenario. First, let's pick up the trail of a female Sasquatch at some point in her young adult life. She's lived in a small family group with her parents since infancy, staying somewhat in the same area (though that area is wide by our standards). Each family has its own stomping grounds, and although family groups may run into each other from time to time, they haven't yet run into a single male juvenile who is available for her. Mom and Pop Bigfoot know that she's matured and ready to mate. This October, they take her on a journey, far from their usual "home", to a box canyon high in the remote mountains. It's an area where creatures from miles around have gathered for centuries, during the winter months, to breed and give birth. She's never been here before, and Mom and Pop haven't been here since she was born. There simply wasn't a reason to make the trek again... until now.

After days, perhaps weeks of traveling, they reach the box canyon. There are dozens of creatures and many family groups milling around. Several females are huge with pregnancy. As newcomers and the winter weather arrive, the canyon fills to capacity.

The box canyon, though high in the mountains, provides caves that will maintain a moderate temperature throughout the winter. Pregnant females find shelter in the caves. Their mates, the parents of breeding-age offspring and even the mature juvenile offspring themselves forage for food for the entire group, providing sustenance for the pregnant females, who cannot hunt and forage. As the infants are born, there is a communal effort to provide food for breastfeeding mothers. In addition, the group provides warm bodies and protection for the vulnerable young offspring.

This is an opportune time for sexually mature offspring to find a mate and breed. By finding a mate at a gathering, the offspring can better their chances of mixing up the gene pool - thereby avoiding birth defects from inbreeding. By copulating during the gathering, pregnancy would be timed "properly" so that the birth would occur during the following year's gathering... thus allowing the pregnant female the advantages of community.

The babies are born one by one, mostly throughout December, January, and February. The infants mature more rapidly than humans do and are ready for travel by April (though not necessarily under their own power yet...). In the early spring, the gathering begins to break up, each family group begins the journey back to their old stomping grounds (perhaps now with a new member or two... either an infant or a mate for their mature offspring). Next year, the pregnant females and their mates (and parents) will likely make the journey earlier, to avoid traveling when she is far along in her pregnancy. Once the infant is born, they may not make the journey again for many years...

Okay, wait a minute, Autumn. Where are you getting all of these crazy ideas?

Native Americans lived in relatively isolated communities and would arrange marriages in order to avoid incest and inbreeding. Why would Sasquatch be any different? With something as important as survival of the species at stake, do you suppose Bigfoot families just "wait around" in hopes that a family with an equally eligible youngster of the opposite sex might happen by? Or would they have developed, long ago, a means by which to facilitate breeding? Are you finding it hard to swallow this idea? Perhaps because you're assuming that they're more gorilla-like and less like, say, a Neanderthal?

So why did I choose the winter months? Why not the summer, when food is plentiful at ALL elevations? Well, for a couple of reasons: First, the time during which it is most difficult for a pregnant female to find food might be the best time to rely on the community to help. Secondly, and most importantly, I have numerous reports from eyewitnesses, both long-term and incidental, that tell of female Sasquatches being seen with young infants predominantly in the spring. In addition, the number of reports of creatures seemingly "passing through" rural areas tends to increase in the spring and fall (those reports which indicate that a creature was moving quickly through an area, was not sighted again, etc.)

So there you have it. Again, please remember that these are ideas, not beliefs. It could also be that the creatures simply stumble around in the woods, bump into one another, breed, and give birth on the fly. I think it's unlikely, simply because the closest model we have to a "Sasquatch lifestyle" is Early Native Americans and they didn't do things that way, for good reason.

(Also, researchers often ponder whether these creatures are "territorial" or "nomadic". Weren't Early Native Americans

both, in a way? They'd choose a spot to inhabit but then would journey occasionally to other areas for a specific purpose...)

One final thought... could you imagine coming across one of those box canyons and seeing a gathering with your own eyes? Wow. Of course, the creatures there might be overprotective and not quite friendly...

I have my ideas about where some of these areas might exist. Where do you think they might be? Why do you think, if the above stories were accurate, these creatures would kidnap humans and bring them into a Gathering Place?

Autumn Williams
August 17, 2006

When I wrote this, I was primarily focused on the idea that Sasquatches (and perhaps Skunk Apes) might gather during a particular season for the purpose of mating or bearing young. Doing so in a communal setting might offer protection and care that would otherwise be lacking to a small family unit. Rather than the adult male being solely responsible for providing food and protection for the pregnant female, any current offspring, and a newborn infant, all able-bodied adults and older juveniles in a communal setting could "pitch in", as it were. But as I was writing, I was imagining groups of these creatures, family units if you will, coming to this place simply for the purpose of communion as well.

(Mike and I had never discussed my breeding grounds article. Nor did he have any idea what I was referring to when I mentioned it after reading his encounter. As far as I know, as I write this book and share it with Mike as I write it, this will be the first time he's ever read this article I'd written.)

When you read what Mike left for me in our "docs" that day, I think you'll understand why I was so floored by what he claimed to have witnessed.

And why he didn't want to tell me before now.

* * * * *

[Editor's note: When asked to give a date, Mike thought this occurred in 2005 or 2006]

It was early October when I saw what I call the Skunk Ape Convention. They were everywhere. At first, I thought I was seeing the same one over and over. But I got to thinking, and to see him every place that I did, he would have to be running all the time.

The Big Guy was taking a lot of food "to go". I had to make more trips to town to get more and it was costing a lot of money.

I decided that I was going to follow him the next time he took food out into the swamp. It was almost sundown when he came into camp and I was ready for him. I had his food in a box, which he took and sat down by the log and ate, and as he ate, I bagged up the rest. I had a big paper bag that you put yard waste in. (They were thick and wouldn't bust open.) I had fruit, bread, nuts, cookies… it was most of the remaining food. I held back a little in case he came back later.

He finished eating and, like always, he lay back against the log and burped, resting his head back, looking up at the sky.

It was getting dark and I wanted him to go so I could follow him. I wanted to see what he was doing with all the food. I set the bag next to him and said, "So, I guess you'll be going now..." He didn't move; he just stared at the sky. I said, again, "You better get going. It's getting dark. Don't want you walking into a tree out there…" Still, he didn't move. He just sat there looking up at the sky. I sat down beside him and did what he was doing. I looked up and said, "What are you looking at up there?" His reply was to cut a huge fart.

I rolled over to get away from the stench. Getting up, I held out some paper towels and said, "Do you want to wipe your butt? You nasty ass old fart." He didn't move... not even a blink of an eye.

By now, the sun was almost down and it was getting dark. I sat down on the cooler and stared at him, not saying a word. After a while, he sat up, looked around, got to his feet and walked to the edge of camp, looking out into the darkness. I think he was waiting for someone. He made a whistling sound and stood there like he was waiting for a reply. He whistled again and this time he got the reply he was waiting for. He whistled back and turned around, picked up the bag, walked over to where I was setting and took his finger and flipped my hat off my head, turned and walked into the darkness.

I waited about two minutes and grabbed my hat and pack and walked out after him. I was walking down a trail and had not gone far when he stepped out from behind a tree and huffed at me. His breath was foul and I almost gagged. I stepped back and said, "Hey, funny running into you out here!" He took his hand and put it on my chest and pushed me backward. I stepped back toward him and said, "I want to know who you are feeding out here. You got a girlfriend out here somewhere?" He turned and started walking and I followed. I took about ten steps and he turned and pushed me back, a little harder this time. I knew better than to push my luck, so I let him go. I had to come up with another plan.

The next morning, I got up early and headed for town to get more food. It was a bright sunny day and I knew I wouldn't see him until late afternoon. I drove by the local feed store and got an idea. I wondered if he would eat cow or horse feed... maybe some sweet pellets. I walked around looking at the different feed and decided on some sweet cow feed. It was in pellets and a fifty-pound bag was only five bucks. If he would eat some of this, it would save me a lot of money; also, I could leave it in a feeder and he would always have something to eat when I wasn't around. I got ten loaves of day-old bread, fruit, nuts, and some vegetables and headed back to the swamp.

When I got back to camp, he was waiting for me. He was standing by the log as I pulled my skiff up to camp. Climbing out of the skiff, I said, "I didn't expect to see you this early. What's up?" He walked up to me and pushed me backward. I stumbled back, almost falling and said, "What the hell you doing?" He looked down by the woodpile and there was a cottonmouth coiled up ready to strike. I would've stepped in striking range if he hadn't pushed me. I pulled my pistol and was going to shoot it and I saw him stepping back with a scared look on his face. "Oh, I forgot. Sorry," I said, and put the gun back in the holster. I picked up the ax, chopped its head off, and threw it in the creek.

"Thanks, buddy... I didn't see that little bastard. He might have bit me. I've gotta be more careful. You hungry? You wanna eat?" I took a loaf of bread, poured cane syrup on it, and handed it to him. He sat on the log and ate it. While he was doing that, I

got some of the cow feed, put it in a big metal pan and walked over to him. "Try this... see if you like it." He sniffed at it, then took a handful and put it in his mouth. He chewed it up and swallowed and took some more. "Hey, Mikey, he likes it!" I said. "Well, I don't know if it is good for you... but it costs a lot less."

I didn't give him too much of it at a time. I was afraid it would make him ill or gain too much weight, so I would put a pound of it in with the rest of his food along with Quaker Oatmeal. He seemed to like it.

I could write a Skunk Ape cookbook... I was always coming up with some new dish for him.

While I was feeding him, I thought I saw something moving out in the swamp. I stopped and looked to see what it was. It was a dark figure moving from tree to tree. I'd seen this before - that's what the Big Guy does when he is being sneaky, but it was too far out to get a good look. I said, "It looks like someone is spying on us. He a friend of yours? What ya say we call him in?"

The Big Guy never looked up from his food. He just kept eating. So I packed some more food - this time in a big cardboard box - and put about ten pounds of the cow feed in with it.

It was around 4:00 p.m. and, when he finished eating, he knelt down and took a big drink from the creek. He stood up and burped. Walking to the edge of camp, he made a yelping sound like he was calling to someone. I handed him the box of food and he left. This time, it was still daylight.

I got my binoculars from the skiff, sat down on the log and watched him walk away, carrying the box under one arm. He got about three hundred yards out - all I could see was from his shoulders up because of the underbrush. Then I saw two more heads pop up, then another. Then they all knelt down and went out of my sight. I guessed they were eating. (That's what they do: they squat down with the food in the middle and help themselves until it's gone.)

I kept watching and a head popped up and was looking around. It was Enoch. I guess he wasn't hungry after eating in camp so it looked like he was keeping an eye out for danger while the others ate.

After about ten minutes, the other heads popped up, one at a time, and they stood around for a few minutes and then disappeared in the underbrush.

I sat there thinking that I had never seen so many Skunk Apes at one time. What the hell was going on... a damned Skunk Ape convention?

Later that night, I sat by the fire, staring at the flames. My thoughts drifted back to my past and the ones I had lost. A deep sadness came over me and the loneliness closed in; I was going to my dark place. I had gone there many times before and knew the trail well.

It had made me retreat to the safety of the swamp, far away from people. I couldn't deal with the world or my pain so I tried to hide from it sitting alone in the darkness. Little did I know that my salvation would walk out of the darkness of that swamp and pull me into the light, giving me a reason to go on. He breathed life back into my lifeless soul, pulling me back from the brink, and I am forever grateful to my big hairy friend.

But feeling the way that I did, I was not in the mood for Skunk Ape bullshit. That night, I was drifting off to sleep when something came flying into camp, hitting the table, knocking things off it. I jumped up and saw another piece hit the ground in front of me. Some asshole was throwing wood at me. I picked it up and threw it back as hard as I could. I picked up the stuff that fell off the table, found that piece of wood, and threw it back. I sat back down and they kept throwing wood at me. I got up and went to the skiff. I got a glass, filled it with gas, walked over by the fire, and waited. Another piece came flying in and I dumped the gas on the fire; the fireball rose into the air with a big roar. I stood in front of the fire and yelled, "DON'T FUCK WITH ME TONIGHT, ASSHOLES!" I could hear them running off like a bunch of sissies. Skunk Ape sissies, I said to myself.

I'd read somewhere about a Cherokee rite of passage where they take a boy into the woods at night and blindfold him. They sit him down on a stump and he has to sit there all night and not move or cry out for help. He can't take the blindfold off until the sun shines through it. When he takes it off, he will be a man. And when he takes it off, he sees his father sitting next to him, and did not know that he had been there all night protecting him from harm.

I got a rag and walked out into the swamp there was a stump a quarter mile from camp. I felt it would do just fine. I had no gun, no knife, no nothing - not even a stick of gum. I was there for them to do what they wanted with me. I was going to show them that I was not afraid of them and they did not need to be afraid of me. I was going to prove to them and myself that I was not afraid.

I folded the rag to make a blindfold, put it on and pulled it tight.

I sat there listening to the sounds of the swamp: the frogs, the distant call of a night bird, the sounds of little creatures passing by, not paying me no mind.

I don't know how long I had been sitting, waiting... but after a while, I heard something coming up from behind. Something big. I could hear it breathing. I sat still, waiting for whatever fate it had in store for me. Then it walked away - maybe a bear checking me out and saw I was a nut but wanted something else. My heart was beating fast, but after a few minutes, I calmed down and was pleased with myself that I did not run away like a sissy Skunk Ape. I was chuckling to myself. I thought about what they must have thought when I poured that gas in the fire.

I was glad the bugs were not too bad; a breeze was blowing through the swamp, keeping them at bay. After a while, I heard something walk right up to me. It was right in front of me, and from the smell, I guessed it was Enoch. He stood there, not moving. I could feel him staring at me. I sat still, not saying a word. He walked around me, trying to figure out what I was doing... then he walked away. I counted his footsteps - there were eight and then silence. I wished he would have stayed; it felt good having him there.

It was late. From the coolness in the air, I guessed around 3:00 a.m. I was tired and was drifting in and out of sleep. I wanted the sun to come up.

Then, I heard something behind me. Then something to my right. Then my left. They were all around me.

I could smell them and hear their breathing. I waited, listening to every sound, not moving. My heart was beating fast and I wanted to run. "Run you fool - get out of there!" my mind was saying. But then a calm came over me - a feeling that I was safe.

My heart slowed down, my breathing went back to normal. I had a feeling come over me that everything was going to be all right. A voice in my head told me to be strong - that the darkness in me would go away and that I would be all right. It told me that I was not alone and to hold out my hands. I slowly lifted my arms out to the side.

I felt someone take my left hand, then my right hand. I could feel the warmth and the strength of the hands holding mine - then I felt hands on my shoulders, gently touching me. I felt safe. I wasn't afraid anymore. Slowly, and one by one, the hands left me. I could hear the footsteps go silent and I was alone again. I sat there with tears running down my face. I felt like a big weight had lifted off me and I could breathe once again.

I must have drifted off to sleep. I was awakened by the sounds of the morning songbirds and I knew it was daylight: I could see the sun shining through the blind fold. I took it off... and there standing in front of me was Enoch.

"Good morning," I said. "I'm glad to see you, my friend. You wanna eat?"

I got up and we walked back to camp. I was starving and ate like a pig.

The days went on. I would walk into the swamp and see Skunk Apes everywhere. You couldn't swing a dead cat without hitting one.

But I noticed they were just passing through, going deeper into the swamp. I wanted to know where they were going, so I packed heavy and followed them, keeping my distance. I went deeper and deeper into the swamp – I'd never been this far before and it was getting harder to get through. As the mud got deeper, so did the water and I found myself up to my neck, wading through snake- and gator-infested swamp. I held my pack over my head until I came out of the deep water.

I climbed up on a deadfall log and rested, looking at my arms. I could see the leeches hanging down, sucking my blood, some so fat they could hardly hold on. These came off easy; the rest, I put salt on and they dropped off. I took off my shirt and pants and got the rest off me - the ones on my back, I had to reach around with my knife and scrape off as best I could. After getting dressed, I looked at the time. It was late. I didn't know how much farther I had to go and I knew I didn't want to wade through this swamp in the dark. I took my hatchet, cut some small trees, and made a platform over the log to sleep on for the night. I chopped a flat area on the log and put mud on it so I could have a small fire: a small comfort in this swamp of no comfort.

It was dark and I had a small fire going. I opened a can of soup, setting the can next to the fire to heat. I put on some dry clothes, hanging the others to dry. I had made a bed from moss and cabbage tree fronds, making sure I had a thick layer between me and the moss to help keep the chiggers from biting (or red bugs, as some people call them). I ate my soup and crackers and went to sleep, waking up at the crack of dawn. I ate some peanut butter and crackers, packed up, put the wet clothes back on, slipped into the water and headed out. I still didn't know where I was going and nobody knew where I was. I was on my own. If I got hurt, I was dead.

Coming out of the water, the land rose up and was, for the most part, dry and thick with trees. It was mid-day and I stopped under a large oak and rested. I was tired, so I took off my boots, dried my feet, and made camp, hanging my wet things on bushes to dry.

You have to make sure you keep your feet as dry as you can, and tend to any open wound or sores at once or you risk infection. This is so important - I can't stress it enough. You have to take care of yourself out there or you could get sick and die and nobody will ever find you. I also want to say when you're in the woods, or this case, a swamp, eat what you can find - not what you brought. If you do this, you have a better chance of surviving longer and you always have a reserve of food.

With that in mind, I went fishing and caught some catfish and cooked them up. I had decided that this was a good place to make a camp, so I built a hut out of cabbage palm fronds to get me out of the weather and bugs... and most of all to keep dry.

The next day, I got up and headed out, looking for any signs of the Big Guys. It was not long before I found some tracks. I followed them deep into the woods, trying to be as quiet as I could.

Through my binoculars, I could see small clearing with knee-high grass and a large black figure standing on the edge of it. It turned and looked right at me and started coming toward me. I stood my ground and waited to see what it would do. I watched it and it vanished right in front of me: he was there one second, gone the next. He had ducked down and was sneaking up on me. I think he didn't know that I saw him. He was watching me, peeking around trees, checking me out. I walked on to the clearing and he followed, thinking I did not know that he was there. In the middle of the clearing I found deer tracks and, on the other side, wild hog tracks. I think he was waiting for a deer or hog to come to feed and would run out of the woods and kill it for food.

I didn't stay long - I didn't want to mess things up for him, so I headed back to camp. They knew I was here now, and all I had to do was go back to camp and wait. They would find me.

That night, I was in camp cooking the gator I had killed on my way back to camp. There was much more meat than I could eat. I hoped that Enoch would find me so I could share it with him. I had no other food to give him, so it would have to do. As it cooked over the fire, I waited. I could hear them out in the woods, walking around, but they wouldn't come in too close.

I was getting ready to go to sleep and I heard a grunt behind me. Turning around, I saw Enoch standing there like a big tree.

"Hey, pal. Long time no see. You wanna eat?" He stepped forward and I got the rest of the gator tail and handed it to him. "Sorry, this is all I got. Maybe tomorrow I can kill a hog."

He took the gator tail and started to eat, taking big bites. It was gone in a few minutes and I said, "That's all I got. If you want more, you'll have to get it yourself."

He hung around for a while, then I looked up and he was gone. No goodbye - just gone. That's right... eat and run and don't worry about a tip. I'm good.

The next day, I went back to the clearing and looked around. Just inside the tree line, I could see a lot of movement. Looking through my binoculars, I could see at least six Skunk Apes moving around, eating leaves, grass, and anything else they could find.

I hid inside a large clump of palmettos and watched them most of the day. They would come into the clearing, eat grass and bugs, and just lay in the sun. I watched them for the next two days. On the third day, I was laying on my belly watching them when something grabbed my foot and pulled me out of my hiding place. I rolled over and it was Enoch standing over me with a strange look on his face. I thought he wasn't happy with me, so I got to my feet and said, "Sorry, Big Guy." I felt stupid; like a Peeping Tom who had been caught peeking in someone's window.

I reached in my pack, pulled out two Blue Birds, and handed them to him, which he ate right down. I took the wrappers and licked the sugar off them. In the woods, that was a treat not to be wasted. I dug a hole with my foot and covered them up.

He seemed to lighten up a bit. He walked to the edge of the clearing, turned, and looked at me. Somehow I knew he wanted me to go with him, so I followed him into the clearing.

When we got to the middle of the clearing, he stopped, and I walked up and stood beside him. I couldn't believe what I was seeing. Skunk Apes. Big ones, little ones... were looking at me from the woods. I think he was letting them know that I was his friend and could be trusted.

I didn't know what to do. I just stood there, dumbfounded. I stepped in front of Enoch to let them get a good look at me. Then I raised my hand and said, "Hello, my friends. I'm Mike. I want to be your friend." I don't think they understood but I felt I needed to say something.

The little ones hid behind their mothers, peeking around from behind, afraid of the human that stood before them. I stood there, taking it all in. I wanted to remember every second because this would never happen again.

I turned around to talk to Enoch and he was gone. I looked around and there was no sign of him. I looked back at the others, waved and walked away, stopping every few feet to take another look. They all watched me go. I stopped at the edge of the clearing, turned around, and waved again and this time I made an Indian call. I turned and slipped into the woods and went back to camp for the rest of the day.

I planned to return the next day. I was going to walk into that clearing alone and see what happened.

I cooked the catfish I'd caught. I ate my fill and saved the rest in case the Big Guy came around, but he did not show that night. It was quiet all night - no sounds of footsteps in the woods. I kind of missed it. I slept good that night; a light rain was falling, so I set up a small tarp to catch the rainwater. I was glad, as I was getting tired of the taste of boiled swamp water. (Even after boiling it, it still tastes like mud, but it will keep you alive.)

The next morning, I ate the rest of the catfish and cooked a small pot of oatmeal sprinkled with brown sugar. I like to eat oatmeal: it keeps me filled up for a long time (plus, I just like it… hey, Mikey…). I had caught almost a quart of rainwater and it was a good and welcome treat. I poured it into my canteen, packed up and headed to the clearing, which was a half mile away. I was nervous; it was like the first day of school. I got to the edge of the clearing around 10:00 a.m. and the ground was still wet from the rain. It was an overcast day. I looked across the clearing and I could see them walking around, eating.

I stepped into the clearing and made that Indian call again to let them know I was there. I waited to see what they were going to do. Nothing. They did nothing. They looked up and stared for a few minutes, so I walked out to the middle where Enoch had led me the day before. I stopped and waved and said, "Good morning, friends, do you mind if I sit awhile and rest?" They just stared at me, so I sat down in the grass and got some nuts from my pack and had a snack. They watched me for a few more minutes and went back to what they were doing, all the time keeping an eye on me.

Over the next few days, I went to the clearing, trying to gain more of their trust. But they kept their distance. The only one who would come to me was Enoch.

I was running out of supplies and I needed to check on my skiff and pickup, so I headed out at sunup. It was a lot easier; I had a lot less to carry.

I had to figure out how to get more supplies to the "Skunk Ape rendezvous". I needed food to entice them to trust me and let me come closer.

I went home for a few days to figure things out and I decided that I would use an inflatable boat to ferry supplies across the deep part of the swamp. It was light and could hold a lot of weight. I spent the next few days hauling supplies to the rendezvous. The food would be the last trip. I got a big tent to put everything in to keep it dry and planned to stay two weeks. I got a man who lived next to the boat ramp to let me park my pickup in his backyard... One less thing to worry about.

Back at the rendezvous camp, I went to work, spending as much time as they would let me watching them. The food was going fast and still I was getting nowhere. I would leave food and when I would come back, it would be gone. They didn't hide when I came around but wouldn't let me get close. I tried day and night... I had better results at night. They would come around my camp but would stay just out of sight. I could see them standing there in the dark but that's all the contact I had. I never quite knew how many of them there were - they would come and go. I couldn't keep track of them, but my guess was around fifteen, give or take one or two.

-15-

SHELBY

One night, I was sitting in camp feeling low because of the lack of progress I'd made.

I looked up and saw Enoch. He was standing at the edge of camp, which was strange... most times he just walked in. But as I looked at him, something was different. He was not alone; he had someone with him.

"Come on in. You wanna eat?" He stood there, and kept looking at the fire, then back at me. I took some water and poured it on the fire, then took a spade and threw dirt on it so it wouldn't smoke.

By the time I got it buried, my eyes became used to the dark and with the almost-full moon, I could see well.

I stepped back and gave them room. He came in first, followed by a female - and behind her was the cutest little girl Skunk Ape. I looked at them, then at Enoch and said, "My friend, you've been holding out on me. Is this your family?"

He was chattering. I think he was proud of them. We all stood there looking at each other, and then I said, "You wanna eat?"

I got some apples and gave them to him. He gave each of them one and took one himself. I was excited - I couldn't believe what was happening. It was all I could do to control myself.

I got some bread, fruit, and shelled walnuts and put it all down on the ground in a box and stepped away. He took the box and they sat down in the middle of camp and had a feast.

The little one was so cute; I couldn't take my eyes off her. She hid behind her mom and peeked around her at me. I'm not good at guessing their age, but I would say she was four to six years old.

As long as they ate, I brought them more. I would reach over Enoch to put it down, to not scare them. And when they'd had their fill, they got up and walked away.

I was so excited I couldn't sleep that night. The Big Guy had a family: that lucky dog, it works for everyone but me.

Over the next few days, he started bringing them around in the daytime just before sundown. They would come into camp and eat, then leave. They were getting used to me and the little one got to where she wasn't afraid at all. She would come up to me and take food from my hand. I called her Shelby and she seemed to respond to it.

The other female was a little smaller than Enoch, but not by much. She carried herself with an air of confidence. She acted almost stuck up. I would look at her and she had the kindest eyes, full of love. She had gentleness in her eyes that made you feel at ease around her: a very non-threatening, sweet soul. I was looking at her one day and I thought, 'She reminds me of someone... but who?'

Then it hit me: Cora Beth Godsey from The Waltons. She acts just like her. I named her Cora Beth.

One evening, as they were just getting ready to leave, I stopped them and gave them all a Hershey bar. Enoch loved them but his family had never had one before and were not quite sure what to make of it. (The first time I gave Enoch one it was before we were friends. I had left it on a log where he would find it. He sniffed it, then licked it, then put it in his mouth. He loved it so much that he started rocking back and forth: he looked like Jerry Lee Lewis rocking out.)

Enoch put the whole thing in his mouth and chewed and smacked his lips. Cora Beth took a bite and almost smiled - you could see it in her eyes. Shelby she took a bite and started jumping up and down but her feet never left the ground. It was the cutest thing; it made her happy and all the hell I went through was worth it just to see that.

As they walked away, I called to her, "Shelby, come here, baby girl." I held out a Hershey bar and she came running to get it. She took it and ran back to her mom, looking over her shoulder as they walked away.

After that, I gave up on trying to be friends with the rest of them. We agreed to live and let live and respected each other's space.

The wood throwing stopped.

(You've asked me time and again if they share things with me or leave gifts. I told you no because I was already telling more than I had wanted to. But if the truth be known, I would have to say yes, they did. In fact, it got to be a problem.)

Enoch would bring me things once in awhile - like the pig he tossed by the fire or a swamp cabbage or a duck or whatever he had killed that day, and that was fine. I would cook it, we would share it, and it was never a problem.

But after a couple of weeks at the rendezvous, I would leave camp and go off to do whatever - and when I got back there would be a dead rabbit or a chunk of deer meat or a swamp cabbage. One time, I found a dead turtle sitting on the ground, the bottom shell torn away. It looked like a big bloody oyster on the half shell, covered with flies. Oh, yeah… I really wanted to just dive in and chow down, pass the ketchup.

Whenever one of them would come back from hunting, he would drop something off at my camp for me. I had to find a way to get rid of these things. After all, it would be rude for me just to throw it out where they could see it, and I didn't want to piss them off. I was walking a very thin line and I wanted to be accepted as one of them. I didn't want to seem ungrateful.

But most of all it would be wrong of me to let the animals who gave their lives so others could live be wasted. It's a Skunk Ape thing: take only what you need to survive and be thankful for it.

So I became a Skunk Ape cook. Yes, that's right. I would take the food they would bring by and cook it and then I would take it to the clearing.

Stopping at the edge of the clearing - most of the time it was after dark - I would make my call to let them know I was there, then I would walk out into the clearing and set the food on the ground and squat down and eat some. Sometimes Shelby would come to me and I would share it with her, then I would reach out and touch her cheek and say, "I got to go, baby girl." By now, I would be surrounded by them. It was really intense, but in a good way. They always left me an opening to walk away when I was ready.

Shelby would follow me to the edge of the clearing, holding my arm, talking up a storm. Then Mom would call and she would take off running back across the clearing.

As I would walk back to camp, two or more would follow me... and when I got into camp, one would whistle and I would see them vanish into the darkness. It was almost like they were making sure I made it back okay, because as soon as I got there, they left. I never felt like I was in danger; in fact, I felt really safe. After all, what would screw with me with bodyguards like them?

I'm only guessing that's why they did it because they were just as likely to run me off for getting too close. But I feel they knew I was bringing food for them and showing my thanks to them for what they gave me. (Or, I could be dead wrong about the whole thing.)

Also, Shelby would make me what I would call a dream catcher - some were round, some square, some would be made up of two or three sticks hooked together like links in a chain. I still have them and wouldn't take all the gold in the world for any of them.

After a few weeks, they had all gotten used to seeing me and wouldn't run and hide when I came around. I still couldn't get too close to them; they would keep their distance. But I would hear them walking around my camp, watching me, staying just beyond the fire light.

When I would walk around at night, I would feel something hit me in the back or touch my shoulder or arm, sometimes knocking my hat off. When I turned around nothing would be there.

Then it started to happen in the daytime - only now I could see who was doing it. It was the little ones, playing games. I think the game was to see who could touch me and not get caught.

They would sneak up from behind, touch me, then turn and run, laughing, and hide in the underbrush. Sometimes I would chase them but they were too fast and were gone before I took three steps.

One day, when I was back in town, I was sitting at a traffic light when some bicycle riders stopped next to me. As I was looking at them, I noticed some of them had little mirrors on their helmets to see behind them. I got an idea, so I stopped at a bicycle shop and bought a set. I was going to turn the tables on them little buggers.

Well, it seemed like a good plan at the time - but like all good plans, some are doomed to fail.

I was sitting in camp waiting for the little ones to come sneaking around, and I had the mirrors ready. After a little while, I could see a young male coming up behind me. He looked like he was around nine or ten years old. When he was about to touch me, I turned around and growled at him. He looked surprised. I guess I scared him really good because he punched me right in the face, knocking me on my butt. My face felt numb and blood was running from my nose and my lip was split and bleeding. I sat there holding my nose trying not to laugh 'cause it made my lip hurt.

He ran off and hid in the under brush and I could hear them chattering with excitement. I got up and got a towel, held it to my face and sat back down. It was funny to me and I couldn't help feeling like Wiley Coyote trying to catch the Road Runner.

Everything I did came back in my face. But I think it made it more fun for them because they knew that I could catch them once in awhile.

The game went on for the rest of the time that I was there and we had some good times. I really miss the little ones. I wish they would have trusted me more. I would have loved to get to know each one of them.

The only one who would come to me was Shelby.

Shelby stood about 5'5" when I first met her. She had big brown eyes: her eyes were a little bigger than her parents' were and her head was smaller, compared to the size of the others. Her body was lean and her hair was short and well groomed. She didn't have the bulky stature of her parents, most likely because of her age. She was shy at first, then quickly took a liking to me. She was well mannered and passive, almost polite in her demeanor. She was a good kid in my book. I grew very fond of her and she would come around a lot and would follow me around. Mom [Cora Beth] was always keeping an eye on her. It was like taking your kid to the park to play with the other kids, and mom would sit and keep a watchful eye out for trouble. I was never allowed to be alone with her. Sometimes, it made me feel distrusted but I understood and wasn't offended. Cora Beth was a good mom and I respected her for that. She was a better mom than some humans.

I would be sitting down on a log and Shelby would come up from behind, put her arms around me, and give me a hug, resting her cheek next to mine. Sometimes, she would hug me too hard and I couldn't breathe. I would have to make her stop before she broke my bones. She was a lot stronger than she looked and would have no trouble beating the hell out of the meanest badass human on this planet. In other words, she would win hands down any

Tough Man match and make them guys cry for their moms. You just gotta love her.

She looked more human than the older ones. In fact, all the young ones looked that way. Maybe just as humans get older and lose their looks, they do the same. (Now that I think about it, they all look their age: some look really old and move around slower and show signs of old age. I never really thought about it until now. They age just like anything else.)

Getting back to Shelby... her feet are about the same size as mine, but a little wider; five toes; white soles; long toenails. She don't smell as bad as the older ones and that could be because of the short hair. You can see all of her ears and they have a fine hair growing on them. Her skin is a lot lighter than her parents' is; it's like a tan – [similar in color to] someone from the South Pacific.

She is very loving and affectionate. If she is sitting next to me, she is touching me in some way. Like putting her foot on mine or leaning against me or holding my arm. But when mom calls, she hits the ground running. Mom only has to call once.

I have seen them show affection for one another. They truly care for each other and their friends.

–16–

RESPECT

As time went on, I came to understand the way they lived. They had small family units, with two adults and one or two young ones.

The females did the child rearing and the male would gather food and bring it to the female if she had a small baby. The little ones learned fast how to forage for food but the adult male would bring deer, hog, fish, and birds - just about anything it could find- and they would share with the others after taking what they needed.

I didn't bring as much food in as I did at the creek camp; it was too hard to get it there. I would only bring enough for Enoch and his family and that was mostly treats like Blue Birds and Hershey bars and some fruit.

There were also females with no mates who had little ones. The males came and went and it was hard to keep track of who was who.

They didn't build shelters; they would find natural cover like cypress heads and palm hammocks that had a thick canopy to shade and hide them and to protect them from the weather. They would make what I would call a nest-like bed made from moss and cedar or cypress leaves. Anything soft. I had to be careful not to get too close to their living areas. The few times I did, I would be chased away, and they only had to tell me once. It was an uneasy trust we all had - one not trusting the other too much, making sure to respect everyone's space. I was a guest in their world: a point they didn't let me forget and would painfully drive home if I forgot.

One day, I heard a scream like I have never heard before and hope never to hear again. It was a heart-stopping scream that made my blood run cold... and it did not stop.

I grabbed my shotgun and ran as fast as I could to the clearing. I felt fear running through my body. I ran toward the scream, not knowing what to expect when I got there.

I stopped at the edge of the clearing, jacking a slug into the chamber of my shotgun. The scream was sending waves of fear through my body, and my heart was beating so hard I thought it might explode out of my chest.

There she was – a female - walking around in circles, holding the lifeless body of her child, its arm dangling down, flopping around as she walked. She kept screaming. It was so loud I could hardly stand it: high-pitched screams that I was sure could be heard for ten miles.

She walked into the woods. The others followed and so did I, keeping my distance and staying out of sight. She walked and screamed and walked for over an hour, walking around in circles like she was looking for something.

She came to a small clearing, not much bigger than fifty feet across, and dropped to her knees. Her screams turned to sobs – loud, heart-wrenching sobs.

I stood there, tears running down my face, trying to see through my binoculars.

Two of the males dropped down and started digging with their hands. Dirt was flying as they dug a bowl-shaped hole about four to five feet deep, eight feet across. Others gathered cabbage palm fronds and they put a layer on the bottom of the hole. The one male, her mate, reached out as if to take the child from her arms and she pulled back, sobbing. After a few minutes, she held the child out and the male took it and laid it on the palm fronds. More fronds were put on top of the child and a layer of cedar was placed on top.

The dirt was raked back in and the grave was filled in. Any excess dirt was spread out in a thin layer so no mound would show.

Then out of the woods walked another male, holding a small oak tree about six feet tall. It had a good root ball and it looked like great care had been taken to dig it up.

The tree was planted in the middle of the grave and leaves were raked over the grave, concealing it. When they were done, you couldn't tell that the ground had been disturbed. The tree looked like it had been there all along.

She sat sobbing. One by one, they walked into the woods and she was left to grieve alone.

Her mate waited at the edge of the woods. Slowly, she stood up, still sobbing, and walked to him. He held her arm and guided her into the woods.

I waited about an hour, until I was sure they were all gone, and went to get a closer look at the grave. If you didn't know it was there, you could not have found it.

That tree is a lot bigger now and I always stop and pay my respects when I'm there.

"I could take you right to that tree," Mike said to me one day over the phone. He had just finished relating the story to me again and his voice was gruff, trying to overcome the embarrassment of his tears. He had broken down crying during the telling. "But I won't. If any of them Bigfoot researchers knew about it, you know what they'd do."

Of course I knew. They'd want to dig it up.

A researcher would see it as an opportunity for proof. But to Mike, it was simply a child's grave: deserving of all of the respect that we would afford the body of a human child and a grieving mother's wish that it remained undisturbed.

And there, again, is the separation between witness and researcher that so many researchers have a hard time fathoming. A witness is just that. They witness. Mike was there to watch, and was careful not to interfere – and that very lack of interference, I feel, was crucial to his ability to gain the trust of these creatures, which in turn allowed him to witness all that he did.

Mike simply played the role of a good neighbor. He didn't irritate his neighbors, didn't interfere with their lives, didn't attempt to insinuate himself into their daily routine. He just watched, maintained a healthy distance, shared with them, and *respected* them. And his behavior was consistent. I would soon come to learn just how important this concept was.

Why did I believe him? Because I've gathered, from years of talking to long-term witnesses, that these ingredients are key to developing the trust and rapport necessary to interacting with these creatures.

So why hadn't any of my other witnesses had the same kind of "luck" that Mike had?

As I began to examine this question seriously, I found myself better able to appreciate the Perfect Storm of events Mike repeatedly referred to that caused his success.

First, most of my long-term witnesses' experiences occurred at their homes. In other words, the creatures would gradually approach the witness' homestead and interact with them within the boundaries of human habitation. Not the other way around. In Mike's case, he had stumbled into *their* backyard, and they had a choice – either accept him, or force him out. He had an ambassador, in the form of Enoch. Rather than being chased away, they tolerated his presence. Consequently, he was in the perfect setting to observe them behaving naturally; not as skunk-apes-doing-what-they-do-when-they're-around-humans, but skunk-apes-living-their-everyday-lives-despite-a-human-presence.

I also came to realize that Mike was in a unique frame of mind when he began interacting with Enoch. Having experienced intense, multiple tragedies in his life and feeling the effects of those, he was beyond fear. The memories and emotional pain that made up the personal "demons" he'd mentioned fighting so many times were infinitely more disturbing and frightening to him than any Skunk Ape.

After he related the rendezvous story again to me, I asked him what compelled him to go wading through sometimes neck-deep swamp water infested with alligators, poisonous snakes and leeches, when he appeared to be more than adequately swamp savvy and was well aware of the dangers.

"I didn't give a shit," he told me. "What more did I have to lose? You've got to understand that I was in a very dark place in my life. I was wrestling with my demons. I look back now and realize that I did some really stupid things that could have gotten me killed. But I didn't care. Not back then. You wouldn't see me doing half of that stuff now… but I'm in a very different headspace now."

It also occurred to me that Mike's behavior was consistently respectful. He was respectful of their space, the "food" items they left for him, their boundaries.

But the final light of understanding dawned during one of our many phone conversations, in which we discussed his opinion on films, images, sounds and eyewitness testimony; including, "The Creature" by Jan Klement.

-17-

UNIQUE INSIGHT

I asked Mike to take a look at a couple of things and give me his opinion. Suddenly, he was irritated with me again. "I ain't no expert."

"I know," I said patiently, grinning. "But you've had more opportunity to observe these guys than anyone I know. I'm just curious to get your take on these things."

I asked him to look at the Patterson/Gimlin Film[1] again, and sent him a link. "What do you think?"

"Whaddaya mean, what do I think?" he asked, still a little pissy with me. "What do *you* think? You've seen 'em. That's how a Bigfoot moves. That's what a Bigfoot looks like. You know that. Why are people running around bitching about wanting a picture? They've got one."

He didn't have much else to say about Patty until I was trying to create the artwork for the cover of the book. We went back and forth, me sending him images and files of my attempts to depict Enoch just right and Mike getting more and more frustrated.

"Look, I told you. This is what he looks like: his head's a little pointed – not like all those cone-heads people draw all the time. His ears stick out sometimes, just the tips, when his hair's messed up a certain way. He's got big bushy eyebrows, like Andy Rooney. His eyes are dark brown… you ever eat a Tootsie Pop? A chocolate one? You know

---

[1] A clear digitized version of the Patterson/Gimlin film is available in the supplemental section of the DVD, <u>Sasquatch: Legend Meets Science</u>, Whitewolf Entertainment

how you get down about halfway, and you can see the Tootsie-Roll center? It's… what's the word…?"

"Striated?" I asked, tickled by his comparison.

"Yeah. Striated. Like that."

I asked about the pupils.

"His pupils are like ours; depending on the amount of light, that's what size they are. If it's dark, they get real big. If there's a lot of sunlight, they get smaller, but then he's usually squinting. His eyes are all brown. The only time I see any whites is when he looks way off to the side. You know, like a dog's eyes. But his eyes are deep."

"Intense?" I asked.

"Yeah. Especially when he's staring at me for a long time like he does. It's almost like he's getting ready to say something."

"Ok," I asked. "What else?"

"His nose is kind of broad and flat, but not like a gorilla's with those big nostrils. He's got these little pig bristles that stick out from it. And wrinkles. On the bridge, and down a little farther, too. His mouth is wide and his mustache is real thick, like it grows almost out of his nostrils. It covers his upper lip. His teeth are wide and flat. His beard grows all the way up to his cheekbones, but is a little sparser as it goes up. His mustache grows down the sides of his mouth and blends with his beard. His beard has kind of a goatee, a Fu-Manchu thing hanging down, about six inches long. His forehead has sparse hair on it that blends up into his hairline."

I sent him drawing after drawing. None of them was close to Enoch.

"Ok, it's easy. Look at Patty. See the hair growth on her face? Like that. See the shape of her head? See her face, her nose? Like that. She could be his sister. She's the closest thing to what he looks like. And guess why? *'Cause she's a Bigfoot!"*

I laughed. Fair enough.

Next, I asked Mike to look at the Freeman footage[1].

Paul Freeman, a US Forest Service employee, had a sighting near Walla Walla, WA in 1982. The sighting created such an impression on him that he quit his job a couple of years later and spent the rest of his life searching for the creatures. Despite murmurs of hoaxing, members of the scientific community, including Dr. Grover Krantz, Dr. Henner Fahrenbach and Dr. Jeff Meldrum, supported tracks cast by Freeman as critical evidence. Jimmy Chilcutt, a fingerprinting expert who had studied the feet and hands of great apes, analyzed dermal ridges on the casts and found them to be inconsistent with any known primate.

In 1994, Freeman was following a series of tracks near Deduct Creek when he filmed a bulky, dark-haired creature. When I was working with producer Doug Hajicek on Mysterious Encounters in 2003, Doug showed me the footage on his big screen high-definition TV. Toward the end of the footage, there is a brief shot of what appears to be an additional creature lifting a juvenile. The feet and legs of the tiny creature were clearly visible on the high-definition screen, ankles articulating. According to Doug Hajicek, Freeman had never mentioned the juvenile to him, and Hajicek told me he didn't think Freeman was even aware that it was in the footage. Freeman passed away from complications of diabetes in 2003.

When Mike watched the footage (despite the poor quality clip on YouTube, I was able to point out the lifting

---

[1] A clear digitized version of the Freeman footage is available in the supplemental section of the DVD, Sasquatch: Legend Meets Science, Whitewolf Entertainment

of the juvenile toward the end of the clip), he had this to say: "That is what my Big Guy looks like when I see him in the woods, and that is the way he moves. Notice how he looks at [Freeman], then looks at where he is going, then back at him. They are very careful where they put their feet so they don't misstep and get hurt. And as far as the little one... it makes sense that Momma would carry her young to get away from danger - or some dude with a camera."

Next, I asked Mike to look at the Memorial Day footage[1].

Filmed in May of 1996 by Lori Pate on a barren hillside above Chopaka Lake in Northern Washington, the Memorial Day footage appears to show a rather small creature running in the open. It passes behind a small hill briefly. Interestingly, when the creature nears the tree line at the far side of the open area, it raises an arm over its shoulder and seems to *grow* several inches. Again, viewed on a high-definition screen, it appears that it is lifting a small infant onto its shoulders.

Though some researchers question the authenticity of the Memorial Day footage, I've always leaned toward these images being authentic, and Mike thought they might be, too. "All you have to see is the last ten seconds, the way it moves... See the way it runs across the hill? Nothing moves the way they do. Fast and sure-footed."

Next, we turned to the Sierra Sounds[2]. In the early 1970's, Ron Morehead and Alan Berry returned again and again to Warren and Lewis Johnson's hunting camp in the High Sierras, and recorded many close-range, interactive

---

[1] A clear digitized version of the Memorial Day footage is available in the supplemental section of the DVD, Sasquatch: Legend Meets Science, Whitewolf Entertainment

[2] The Sierra Sounds recordings, Volume I and II, can be ordered on CD from www.Bigfootsounds.com

vocal exchanges between what were assumed to be Bigfoot creatures and the men in the camp.

There are a couple of reasons I've personally been a proponent of the Sierra Sounds. I have known Ron Morehead for many years and have found him to be very credible. But more than that, the sounds recorded in that camp closely approximate those descriptions given by many witnesses over the years of close-range vocalizations they've heard.

Since Mike had been in such close proximity to these creatures for so many years, I figured he'd be able to tell me if he'd ever heard anything like these sounds. I sent him several audio tracks via email, and we listened to them together over the phone.

Mike started chuckling. "You hear that really garbled sound he's making right there?" he asked.

"Yeah."

"Enoch does that all the time. He'll be sitting next to me in camp, eating, and our conversations will go something like this:

'How you doing today, buddy?'

'Blurg raggle bleg.'

'Really? Well, why is that?'

'Bragga blech ragga ruuur.'

'She did that to you? What did you say?'

'Agga rug blag blagga racka mrrrg.'

'Well, I hope you told her off.'

I laughed. Mike's approximation of the Sierra Sounds was eerily accurate.

"It's like when you sit and have a conversation with your dog or something. You're talking nonsense and they're making noise in response. Lots of times, though, when they're interacting with each other, it sounds almost like a Native American language. Do you ever watch those old Western movies, where the Indians are speaking to one another in their language? It reminds me of that."

We continued listening to the tracks I sent him, and he stopped on Track 09. This track has always been of particular interest to me because the sounds are better-formed and sound more like language than gibberish.

"There," Mike said. "Do you hear that?"

That was a particular piece of the recording in which the creature was forming what sounded like commands in an authoritative voice.

There was silence on the other end of the phone. I wasn't expecting what came next.

"Shit," Mike said, and barked a short, almost hysterical laugh.

"What?" I asked.

"Awww, shit," he said again.

"What?"

He blew out a breath. He sounded rattled. "This is really weird…" Silence. Then came another of Mike's explanatory metaphors. "Sometimes, I'll be standing around at work and the Mexican guys will be speaking to each other in Spanish. I don't speak Spanish, but I'll grasp what they're saying without even realizing it and interject something into the conversation." He hesitated. "I think I just understood what he said."

It was my turn to get quiet.

"What did he say?"

I could tell Mike was struggling with this. "Well… it sounded to me like he was upset. The men are mimicking him, repeating what he's saying, like it's a game, but he's shouting in anger because the men are… in between… him… and something that matters to him."

I didn't know what to say.

Strangely and coincidentally (though the longer I'm on this Earth, the less I believe in coincidence), I had an opportunity to speak on the phone for the first time about a week later with Dave Johnson, the son of the man who owned the hunting camp.

During our two-hour conversation, I thought about what Mike had said, and asked Dave a subtle but pointed question.

"You know on Track 09, when the Big Guy is shouting out what sounds like words? What was going on in camp that night?"

Dave told me, "The guys thought that one of the younger ones had gotten over on the other side of the camp and they were between it and the rest of them."

* * * * *

Mike was unknowingly helping me put pieces of the puzzle into place, one by one. Pieces that had been sitting on my desk for years, gathering dust; pieces that had seemed compelling yet had no real useful context before now.

The more I learned of Mike's story, the more I was reminded of a similar story I'd read years before. A small book, "The Creature: Personal Experiences with Bigfoot" by Jan Klement[1] was published under a pseudonym and the author's identity has never been revealed.

"The Creature" tells the supposedly true story of this man's encounters with a Sasquatch-type creature he

---

[1] Jan Klement, The Creature: Personal Experiences with Bigfoot, 30th Anniversary Reprint Edition (Elgin, PA: 2006)

befriended in southwestern Pennsylvania at his remote cabin in the woods. Kicked out of his house by his wife due to an "indiscretion", Klement began to stay at the cabin alone.

Klement's first sighting occurred on a late August afternoon. He had just finished working on digging a pond, and retired to the porch to drink a beer. The creature was crouched near the porch and dashed away into the brush when Klement reacted.

Soon, however, Klement was able to entice the creature in with food offerings and study the creature at length on numerous occasions.

He called the creature "Kong" due to its size.

What follows in the book are detailed descriptions of the creature's appearance and behavior, the author's interactions with the creature, and the subsequent demise and burying of Kong in an undisclosed location.

When I first read the book, I didn't know what to make of it. Klement's description of the creature made it seem slow, or perhaps a little stupid - and, honestly, I felt slightly incredulous due to the rather animal-sounding description of it. It didn't gel with other reports I'd gotten from long-term witnesses that alluded to Sasquatch being a more intelligent, human-like creature.

However, when Mike began to share details of his encounters with Enoch with me, I was struck by how similar many of the details were to those related by Klement. The physical description of the creature, eating habits, behaviors… even the living situation, concerns for the creature's safety and subsequent difficulties of keeping the experience to himself were similar. Many of the parallels were startling.

A phone call I made recently to John Tomikel, the publisher, has lent even more credibility to the Klement story. I called to ask his permission to quote the book here, and what followed was a rather lengthy and pleasant conversation.

I asked Tomikel if he knew the author personally. He said he did. When I asked him what he thought about the book, his answer was candid. He told me that he found "Klement" to be a very credible man, and a scientific-minded one, but said that he had mixed feelings about the book. When I asked why, Tomikel told me it wasn't because of Klement's credibility – he just didn't know whether he personally believed in Bigfoot.

When asked if Klement had ever expressed an interest in anything else "strange" or written any other books on anything like this, he said, "No. He'd written three other books, all very scientific, about forest and swamp animals, the natural world…" He also explained to me, when I asked who owned the rights to the book, that his publishing company did. He had since it was published. He had paid Klement $300 when he handed over his story, mainly to cover the author's expenses for travel and hiring a typist.

"So he wasn't in it for the money?"

"No," Tomikel replied. "He never made a dime on it past that $300 I gave him."

"And he certainly wasn't in it for the fame…"

Tomikel laughed. "'Anonymous' fame? No."

"Huh," I said. I was finally finding more context for the book's credibility.

"You know," Tomikel continued, "when his cabin was torched, we went up there soon after."

"So he really did have a cabin?"

"Yeah," he replied.

I asked Mike if he'd ever heard of the book. He hadn't.

I copied the text of the book from an online source and posted it in our private online documents so Mike could read it and make notes. His comments, written sporadically in bold red at the end of one paragraph after another, were insightful.

For instance, Klement wrote: *"I knew that the paltry food I offered could not support the body of such a huge creature and his diet puzzled me. It was partially explained by the event which I shall relate. I will tell this story now even though it occurred much later in time. It was evening and Kong and I were squatting in front of the porch staring at each other when a young deer appeared off to the side of the cabin. It was the first one I had ever seen on my property. It spotted us and shot up the road toward the top of the hill. Kong leaped to his feet and was off like a flash of lightning. His speed was fantastic as he ran the deer down before it got more than a hundred feet away. He picked it up in his powerful hands and slammed it to the ground, I assume killing it instantly. Instead of returning to me he put the deer under his arm and stalked off through the brush. I did not see him again for five days."*[1]

Mike's response to this: "[It was] because he became a food source, and the deer gave the Big Guy all he needed to survive and [he] did not need the man. Seen that... if there was no food, he would not come around as much. They don't have time to be social and sit around and shoot the breeze. If you don't feed him, he will feed himself."

On some points, it seemed Mike disagreed with Klement. Regarding communicating with the creature,

---

[1] Jan Klement, The Creature: Personal Experiences with Bigfoot, 30th Anniversary Reprint Edition (Elgin, PA: 2006), p. 16

Klement wrote: *"In about three weeks I taught him some commands that seemed to be necessary. He learned to STAY by my giving threatening gestures and holding him with repetition of the word over and over. I would put my arms around his chest and arms and press him downward and say STAY STAY in the early training. He finally got the idea. I had tried rewarding him with apples but he seemed to make no connection with the apples and the performance of the deed. I always tried to use the word STAY with my arm extended fingers out with palm down."*[1]

Mike replied: "You can do this but I have found its more 'monkey see, monkey do'. If you gesture enough, he seems to understand what you want, but it takes a long time. Again, you have to do the same things over and over - then one day he will do it. Like the night he got that one chasing me to leave me alone: he touched his chest and put his hand out to me and walked away."

And, on some points, Mike agreed. *"[Kong] did not seem to grasp the meaning of YES or OKAY because he had no need for asking permission. In the world of nature, the creatures take what they want or do what they wish and are only deterred by superior force or logic. Therefore, he did not need to ask me if it was okay to eat an apple. If he had an apple in his hand and wanted to eat it he would do. If I took an apple away from him and he wanted it back I was not in any position to prevent this."* [2] To this, Mike commented: "I could have not said it better. He does what he wants when he wants. 'No,' or 'May I?' are not in his vocabulary."

---

[1] Jan Klement, The Creature: Personal Experiences with Bigfoot, 30th Anniversary Reprint Edition (Elgin, PA: 2006), pp. 37

I found it particularly fascinating that both Mike and Klement had described the creatures staring for long periods of time.

Klement wrote: *"In our many hours of just squatting and looking at each other there seemed to be no purpose on his part. He seemed to anticipate that I would devise something or do something to give him something. It does not seem strange to me that we would sit and look at each other for hours... The longest Kong and I stared at each other was probably two and a half hours. I do not want to give the impression that this went on in marathon fashion with a massive stare down. I would just study him for about a half hour and then do some little work around the cabin and go back to the spot and Kong would still be there ready for another half hour session. His patience was remarkable. These sessions seemed to produce a hypnotic trance on him but when I would move it would break the spell and he would shuffle. While in the staring state he would appear to be immobilized but then all of a sudden he would move and break this spell."*[1]

Mike's reaction to this: "[Enoch and I] do this all the time. It's like he is staring into your soul, not moving for hours. Sometimes I wonder if he is sleeping with his eyes open. It is kind of like a trance he goes into or maybe one of the sleep stages before you fall asleep. I think there are three stages of sleep in people… why not them?"

Klement mentioned that he thought the smell of his sweat is what first caused Kong to approach. Mike commented: "…When I go to the woods, I don't take a real bath for days, even weeks, when I'm out there. I did not want any unnatural smells on me, and when I would jump in the river to wash, he won't get as close to me. That's why

---

[1] Jan Klement, The Creature: Personal Experiences with Bigfoot, 30th Anniversary Reprint Edition (Elgin, PA: 2006), pp. 38-39

I recommend people not to wear stuff that smells. I don't even wash my clothes with soap - only hot water. I wash my feet so as not to get fungus and my crotch so not to get a rash, but no soap, no nothing. When in the woods, you need to smell as natural as you can. No matter how bad the smell gets."

When Klement wrote of Kong not liking citrus (this was one of the small details that had initially reminded me of this book, since Mike had mentioned this to me in one of our many conversations), Mike said: "He will only eat citrus if there is nothing else to eat, and makes funny faces like it's sour or too tart. It helps to take the peel off citrus - there is a lot of acid in it and I think it burns his mouth. I know it does mine."

Mike agreed with Klement that the creatures are savvy about not leaving footprints, as well. Klement stated: *"He did not show on rainy days, or when the ground was very soft and wet..."*[1] Mike responded: "When the ground is soft or wet he tends to walk off the trails and even steps over a trail when crossing it. Or if humans are in the area he will stay off the trails."

But perhaps one of the most interesting parallels were the similarities in how each man felt about betrayal of the creatures they'd befriended: *"I contemplated what to do about divulging Kong's existence and what was to be the future of the creature and our relationship. I couldn't keep him to myself very much longer and yet I hated to expose him to the world not of his own choosing. It was a feeling, as I recall, like I was about to*

---

[1] Jan Klement, The Creature: Personal Experiences with Bigfoot, 30th Anniversary Reprint Edition (Elgin, PA: 2006), p. 12

double-cross an old and trusted friend although I had only been acquainted with him about six weeks up to that time."[1]

Mike shared that sentiment. "This is how I feel. It's like I said: how do you betray that kind of trust? It would be like throwing a baby to the lions. They would tear him apart and there would be nothing left, and what right do I have to do that? How could I live with myself after doing such a thing? And think how he would feel, being betrayed by someone he trusted. Put yourself in his place and think about it."

Mike and I discussed the book during our next phone call. I asked him, given his own experiences, whether he thought the book was a true account. His answer surprised me. "I think it's true, yeah. I don't agree with everything he said. Like when he was talking about not bathing, and said that was what attracted the creature. When I go out into the swamp, I don't use detergent, deodorant, or anything that smells unnatural. I wash with water and let my natural smells take over. But this guy said that he thought that Kong came around after he'd been digging all day because he was sweaty. I don't think that's why."

Mike stopped in mid-thought and digressed. He posed a question to me, as he often does, trying to get his point across like a patient teacher, making the student think. "When he was out there every day digging, what did he do when he was done? He went inside, got a beer, and set on the porch. The next day, when he was done digging, what did he do? He went inside, got a beer and set on the porch. It's him doing the same thing, over and over again, that made Kong come around, I think."

---

[1] Jan Klement, The Creature: Personal Experiences with Bigfoot, 30th Anniversary Reprint Edition (Elgin, PA: 2006), p. 45

"Because he was *predictable*," I murmured, the realization of what Mike was saying dawning on me, the student finally catching up to the teacher.

"Right. They like to know what you're gonna do…"

"…Because it allows them to feel in control!" I blurted, finishing his sentence.

"You got it." Mike sounded pleased. "It's the repetition. It's not enough just to go out there and do what you do. You have to do the same things every time. They'll sit back and watch you. And when they realize that that's what you do and that's all you're gonna do… they'll feel comfortable enough to come in."

For years, I had been preaching the need for researchers to go out into the woods and simply act like people instead of sneaking around like guerillas wearing camo and ghillie suits. I had stressed the need to behave in ways that were curiosity provoking and non-threatening, of going out in the dark when the creatures would feel most safe. I thought I had grasped the importance of allowing them to remain in control. But all along, I had been missing the one piece of the puzzle.

Repetition.

I understood. It was the *repetition*, the patience necessary to sit on a log or hang around in camp, doing the same things, day in and day out, behaving *predictably*, that would cause these creatures to feel safe enough to approach.

It was a simple formula.

Repetition equals predictability. Predictability equals control. Control equals trust.

I thought about it a minute. "No wonder researchers haven't had any luck," I said. "Most of us are weekend warriors who don't have the luxury of spending that kind of time in the woods. And when we do go out there, we feel rushed; our heads are wrapped up in whatever agenda we have, whatever it is that we hope to accomplish. Our behavior is ruled by that agenda and we push for things to happen."

Something else became clearer in that moment. These creatures were approaching long-term witnesses who experienced repeated encounters at their homesteads because *they had likely been observing the witness over a long period of time.* The Sasquatches watched them, got to know their behavior and schedules. The witnesses were predictable.

I thought about Jane Goodall. Dian Fossey. Their presence in the forests and jungles always amounted to the same thing. Sitting quietly. Watching. Waiting. Daily. Their behavior was predictable as well.

But these creatures, according to Mike, weren't merely apes. I steered the conversation back to the part of Klement's book that had bothered me.

"Was it just me," I asked, "or did Kong seem particularly stupid?"

"You mean, was he like mentally retarded?" Mike was silent for a moment. "Actually, I think he was ill," he said quietly. "I think maybe he had something that was terminal. At least, that's what it sounded like to me." I thought about that for a moment and it made sense. Klement had alluded to Kong's health deteriorating, and near the end of the story, he had found Kong dead.

When I'd reread The Creature, despite the fact that there were many similarities in Klement's and Mike's stories, I was struck by how differently the two men approached the subject. Klement proclaimed that he was "scientifically trained"… and it showed. Much of his discourse on Kong was rather dry and analytical. Mike's was relaxed and observational. I thought again about how witnesses interpret their experiences through their own outlook on the world, and how that can color not only the way a witness relates their experiences, but perhaps the experiences themselves. In other words, Klement couldn't help interacting with Kong as a scientist. Mike, on the other hand, approached Enoch as a friend. That would likely explain the ultimate differences in the level of interaction between the two men and their creatures. It was the difference between thinking and feeling.

It was the difference between the head and the heart.

Mike's comments to me at the end of the Klement story said it all:

Hunger, loneliness, the longing for companionship, the need to feel safe and loved can bring two different things together, one taking what it needs from the other to survive; forming a bond that can last a lifetime, a bond that goes beyond love or friendship. The giving of oneself. A trust. A connection that breaks the chains that would normally keep them apart. Being as different as they are, deep down the two are the same. They come to understand and trust one another and that, my friend, is something that comes around once in a lifetime, and most times never at all. How can you betray a trust such as that? How can you put a price on a friendship that goes beyond all others?

This is very disturbing to me and it has given me pause for thought and reflection about the last ten years. I understand how he felt and why he did what he did, and I see a lot of what I did in this story. It is a burden to carry alone and alone is the only way you can do it. I gave up a big piece of my life over this and have paid a high price for the knowledge I have.

I believe this story to be true as I feel the same way he did: it becomes your life and takes a lot away from you, and replaces it with knowledge you cannot share. I have become more withdrawn from life and people because of it. To have a secret like this and to live a secret life that nobody knows about takes a lot out of you. You learn the art of deception and you tend to stay away from people who might find you out. You lie to family and friends about what you are doing, and along the way you lose respect for yourself.

Don't get me wrong: I would not trade the world for his friendship and trust. I just wish it did not have such a big price tag.

Looking forward, I wonder what will become of me and him. I think he is where he wants to be and, for the most part, as happy as a Big Guy can be. Me, on the other hand? I am not happy and I am not where I want to be and ever since the day I opened this can of worms it has gotten worse. I wish it would go away and leave me be.

When your Big Guy finds you, only then will you know what's in your heart and what kind of person you are. I think most people will be surprised to find that they really never knew themselves at all. It is a humbling feeling to know that you have the lives of a whole species in your hands and one wrong move could destroy them all. I have become paralyzed, not knowing what to do. If I come forward and tell what I know, I'm afraid it will be the beginning of the end for them. I just wish people would leave them alone and let them choose what and who they want in their lives.

This book [The Creature] should be the Bigfoot researchers' bible and they should study it and try to understand why it is more important that they not be discovered. Or maybe you have to have one in your life to fully understand what [Klement] was trying to tell us and why he did what he did in the end. I think that everyone who has ever had an ongoing relationship with these creatures comes to realize that they can never tell.

I believe the bond becomes too strong and they want to protect them, not exploit them... and that is why nobody comes forward.

When one is caught or killed, it will be by someone who only wants the fame of being the one who found Bigfoot. But they've already been found many times. Some call him friend and those are the ones who truly understand. Those are the ones who won't betray the trust, the bond that they have, and that is, for the most part, why they stay in the shadows.

I think that the old saying, "To know him is to love him" rings true. Once he becomes a part of your life, you come to understand what he is and you see the humanity in the beast.

If you ever get to look into his eyes, you, too, will understand. With this comes the burden of having a secret that you can never tell - for what is a secret to me is <u>life</u> to them.

-18-

TESTING THE WATERS

Reading eyewitness stories in my inbox and speaking with witnesses now, I found that I had begun to look at the encounters differently: more from the perspective of the creature that was sighted, rather than that of the witness. Slowly but surely, my paradigm was shifting. However, there was a downside to this: suddenly, I was having a very difficult time doing what I'd always done. I simply couldn't talk about Bigfoot anymore. I couldn't share what I was learning.

Finally, tentatively, I had asked Mike if he would allow me to include his stories in a book, promising to keep his identity and the location confidential.

I didn't know any other way to put this epiphany into perspective for those who were sitting, waiting for the next blog, the next web update. How could I share my thoughts about this subject when I felt I'd taken such a leap forward, without sharing the reason in context?

Mike agreed to the book. "You have to understand, Autumn, that I will not give you any proof to publish. I can't do that to Enoch."

I understood. We had both come to the conclusion along the way that there was no way to prove his existence and provide protection for him in the process.

Nevertheless, I was stuck and didn't feel I had any other choice. I had to do something to put this in context so I could move forward. Now *I* was the one wanting to get it off my chest. And I didn't feel that putting it out there bit by bit on the blog would provide that context. People would read one entry, but not another, and completely miss a piece of the whole. It was the whole that had shaped me – Mike's experiences, the way he related them, and my interactions with him.

I started writing. When I finally stopped to take a breath, I began to think seriously about how the book might be received by the research community and the public. How would my peers react if I decided to publish Mike's story? Would they see the value in it that I did; as simple anecdotal evidence? Since Mike wanted to remain anonymous, would I be able to communicate the impact of Mike's demeanor and credibility, as I perceived it? Would they be able to accept the story at face value without demanding "proof"?

Extraordinary claims require extraordinary evidence...

The phrase, smugly recited by every "serious" researcher impatient with anything that didn't constitute hard, physical evidence rang in my head, an irritating litany.

Knowing the research community as I did, I was well aware that I'd be setting myself up for a firestorm of criticism for publishing Mike's story, knowing full well that I could not - would not - ask him to provide corroborating evidence that he was not comfortable providing. How could I explain to these people that Mike felt uncomfortable talking about it at all – as if he was betraying the trust of a close friend? Would they be capable of appreciating that Mike not only had interacted with a Skunk Ape at close proximity on numerous occasions, but had developed a bond with this particular individual that made him feel adamant about protecting him... and that providing photographs or physical evidence would feel exploitive? They would clamor for proof that he would not provide. Would they understand – and believe – the difference between *could not* and *would not*?

The first issue I needed to address was whether there were enough people out there who would benefit from the book in order to justify putting myself in the line of fire by publishing it. Had I been in this field long enough - developed enough credibility - that people would be able to trust my judgement and suspend their own disbelief long enough to get it?

I thought so, but I wasn't sure. I'd been sitting here for months, with this ever-increasing feeling of frustration, as if the secret to the Universe had been shared with me. Mike had even said that it was all right for me to share it with others… if I had the courage. Whether they'd believe it or not was another thing entirely.

It was time to test the waters.

I posted the following to my blog:

January 19, 2010

I wish I could explain the things that are going on right now.

A few months ago, something happened that changed my life, changed the way I look at this phenomenon. It has affected me deeply and I'm not sure I know which way to turn.

Because all of you have been with me since the inception of this blog, and some of you have been by my side as members and friends much longer than that, I feel the need to reach out to you now and ask for your input.

If I'm vague, I'll apologize in advance. I can't be more specific right now.

I feel that I have learned more about these creatures in the last few months than I have in twenty years of research. The question is, now what? What do I do with this information? The fine line that I've always walked between education and protection has turned gossamer-thin, and I'm struggling to keep my footing.

Let me pose a scenario and ask you a question. Maybe several. This isn't rhetorical; I genuinely want to hear your thoughts.

Those in the research community always talk about providing proof as protection. In fact, I did an extensive blog series on this subject a while back. I've concluded, after much consideration (understatement of the year here), that proving that these things exist will force the hand of the government… and I don't see any good coming of that. First, they'll want to study them (funding will be a major issue and more likely than not the government will do everything in its power not to acknowledge their existence because funding for other projects is an issue now). After studying them, they'll want to harvest one. If it is a male that is harvested first, a female will follow, or visa versa. Will they end up in zoos? I don't know – but I don't want to risk it.

I've never been in this to prove that Bigfoot exists. My goal is, and has always been, to understand and to educate. To validate witnesses who have been ridiculed and give them some peace. To provide support for those who, like me, experienced something they couldn't explain and want to understand. And to protect the very creatures I study.

The question of protection is a funny one. Who do we need to protect Bigfoot from, anyway, besides those who are hell-bent on proving they exist and want to shoot one in order to do so? No one else is deliberately hunting these things. Despite the argument that many make, that "we have to harvest one in order to prove they exist so we can protect them", I've always seen this pathetically altruistic argument as nothing more than thinly-veiled blood lust made more palatable by smearing it with a politically-correct agenda.

Most of you – the vast majority, from what I've gathered – are simply curious, like me. What are these things we call Bigfoot? What do they look like? How do they act? Are they more "human" or "animal"?

And here lies the conundrum:

If I felt I could answer those questions, would you want me to?

If I could offer you detailed observations that would demonstrate the answers, would you care to hear them?

Now… before you answer, keep in mind that there is a caveat here.

Would you still want this information, knowing that I will NOT provide you with anything that will constitute "proof", because I'm afraid of what would happen if I did? Will you allow me to appease your curiosity while protecting the subject of your interest?

Will you allow me to walk that fine line and take the information for what it's worth... or will you demand its head on a stick so that the government can tell us what we knew all along?

Send me your thoughts.

[Edited to say: Please allow me to clarify, since I'm getting some confusing feedback. I WOULD NOT BE PRESENTING PROOF IN THE FORM OF PHYSICAL EVIDENCE. Only detailed observations from a particular witness.]

The response was overwhelming. I received hundreds of emails that day. Of them, only two were critical of bringing forth anecdotal evidence without proof. The majority of readers replied that they already believed that these things existed. They simply wanted to understand them.

I shared many of the responses with Mike and he was taken aback. Until now, his only exposure to the Bigfoot community had been the few websites he'd visited and certain YouTube channels, in which he'd seen researchers going about it in all the wrong ways and patting one another on the back for seeking and finding proof, even if their "proof" only consisted of bent and broken trees or recordings of "wood-knocking". In fact, he had ranted to me once, in writing, about his frustration with the Bigfoot community:

What the hell is wrong with Bigfoot researchers?

Question: If nobody has seen Bigfoot knock on trees, how do they know they do it? Nobody has seen these Bigfoot knocking on trees but they guess they do. So why does that make it fact? A theory is just a fancy name for a guess. The guess that they knock on trees, becomes the theory that they knock on trees, becomes the fact they knock on trees. The fact is, nobody knows for sure.

So when did the guess become theory and the theory become fact?

If you swallow a guess and shit a theory, does that make it a fact?

My theory is that a Bigfoot researcher swallows a guess then regurgitates it a few times to other Bigfoot researchers. Then, while it's still hot, one of the Bigfoot researchers eats the regurgitated guess and pukes up a theory. Then another researcher eats the theory, savoring every factless drop, then - somewhere in his colon - it changes into a fact, which he shits. He then takes this big turd and puts it on his website so all the other ones like him can see it. And they all marvel at how smart he is even though he has never seen a Bigfoot himself. Then, they copy it and put it on their websites next to all the other regurgitated crap they call "Bigfoot facts".

So my question is this: When a Bigfoot researcher shits a fact, does it stay a fact forever, even when there is evidence to the contrary or no evidence to support it?

Mike had said more than once that he'd never seen or heard any of the Skunk Apes in his area knock on trees. While he had allowed for the possibility that they simply may not do that in his area and that others may, he often used the "tree-knocking" subject to epitomize his frustration with the rampant assumptions he felt researchers often made about Bigfoot's nature and behavior… and treated as "fact". I understood Mike's frustration because I had shared it on many occasions. Trying to get the research community to pay attention to long-term witnesses – or anything other than the "accepted" ideas about what Bigfoot is and does - was like trying to pee up a rope.

When I sent Mike the responses from the blog, I wanted him to see the other side of the equation: folks who, like me, had good intentions but who were simply curious, hungry for information; people who weren't so full of themselves and their "importance" as researchers that they would deem his story "a hoax" or his observations fallacious and therefore irrelevant simply because he chose not to exploit the creature he considered a friend by providing photographs, hair samples, spit samples, fecal samples…

If Mike felt obligated to anyone, it was Enoch. But how do you explain this to those who would sit behind their computer screens and condemn witnesses for not being better "researchers"? How do you tell someone that they're lucky to even be hearing the story at all; that the witness was reluctant to share it in the first place with someone that he *did* trust, much less the world at large, and it is only through that delicate thread of trust that he has allowed me to share what is, to him, a deeply personal story?

I hadn't heard from many detractors. But then, most of those folks, I imagined, don't read my blog. I knew what they'd say, though - and a couple of readers didn't disappoint. One commented, "If you're not going to offer any evidence, you shouldn't have said anything in the first place."

Really?

So if a witness agrees to tell you what he's experienced but refuses to provide "proof" that he feels would be exploitive, you're simply going to disregard an entire book's worth of detailed observations and anecdotal evidence that are compelling in every other way? Will you preface every conversation you have with a witness with, "Let me tell you right now… if you're not going to show me all the proof you've got or go out and get it for me no matter what the consequences, I don't want to hear a word you have to say…"?

I learned a long time ago that a lack of respect doesn't get us far in the research field. And it doesn't get us very far in understanding these creatures through the people who experience them. But this hard-line distrust is prevalent in the research field and is part of the reason "Bigfoot research" sits in a rut, spinning its wheels, getting nowhere.

Getting back to the blog responses, the most powerful messages I received from readers were those who said, "I trust you, Autumn. Follow your heart." It seemed that every third response I received contained advice to that effect.

I wanted to. But was my skin calloused enough to deal with the potential lambasting I'd receive from those in the community who couldn't see the forest for the trees? Had I spent so much time in an effort to conduct serious and credible research in this field and earn the respect of my peers only to flush it down the drain by sharing a single, compelling, yet "proof-less" story? Did I have the courage to see this through?

–19–

THE HUMAN ELEMENT

I found myself facing one of the most difficult decisions of my life. I sat down and tried to second-guess all the potential arguments and criticisms, the hair-splitting that would surely occur, not to mention the snide comments and personal attacks that would be lobbed not only at me, but also at Mike.

I kept coming back to the one question that would be foremost in critics' minds.

"If he doesn't want to show us… fine. But have *you* seen a photograph of Enoch? Can you personally vouch that you've seen evidence that his story holds true?"

The answer, still, was no.

I had shared parts of the story with a couple of people that I trusted implicitly, to get their feedback. They were amazed by the details in Mike's account. But they also, invariably, asked The Question… and I had to answer, honestly: "No. I haven't seen a picture."

My explanation that I didn't need a photo to believe Mike, because I felt his reasons for not wanting to provide one were legitimate, sounded like an excuse; a justification for being sloppy and gullible. In other words: a *bad researcher*. Being indoctrinated to the ways of "good research" for so long through the pressure of my peers, bad research – believing without seeing – was an unforgivable sin. In fact, much of the credibility I'd gained over the years stemmed from the fact that I was adamant that I did not "believe" anything about Bigfoot, that I maintained an open-minded skepticism. That we didn't *know* what Bigfoot was. That I sat on the fence and was comfortable there.

Standing in front of the mirror, peering into my own eyes for the truth, I asked myself aloud, "Do I believe him?"

I did.

That answer suited me. It also suited those I'd shared the story with, who trusted my ability to discern truth in eyewitness testimony.

The trouble was, I knew that answer would be completely unacceptable to the research community at large.

I watched the fire of conviction in my eyes sputter and die, replaced by cold frustration as I struggled with the realization that, as a "good" researcher, I could never tell Mike's story without proof. No matter how compelling the story, those who held researchers to a particular standard of corroboration would accept nothing less. My credibility would vanish – and any hope of affecting change within the research community would disappear with it.

I felt frustrated. Sad. Empty. As if it were all for nothing. The more I thought about it, the more I felt painted into a corner. I couldn't go forward. But I could never go back. I couldn't un-ring the bell and unlearn what I felt I had learned.

In a final effort to find some sort of balance, I sat down and wrote an ending to the book, attempting to address all of the potential criticisms.

EPILOGUE

As I said early on, this book is about trust.

I now have a difficult decision to make.

It became clear that Mike didn't feel comfortable providing evidence to back up his claims. From time to time, throughout our saga, we had discussed what might happen if I decided to publish his story without that evidence. He warned me that I would be setting myself up for a fall. I vacillated between feeling he was right, but knowing that this story, if true, was too important not to share.

And now I find myself in a bit of a pickle.

This book was and is incredibly important to me. I finally had a context in which to share what I felt was a valuable message about these creatures whose very existence on this earth has haunted me since I was a child. And I've gotten to the point that I simply cannot move forward in my own work without sharing this story; not just Mike's story – but the affect that it has had on me.

But I'm not stupid. This is my reputation on the line. My credibility. And, in part, my livelihood. When Mike gave me his blessing to write the book, I put everything else on hold. It was that important to me. All the other projects I was working on came to a standstill. While I don't, by any stretch of the imagination, intend to live my days in luxury researching Bigfoot, I have forsaken most everything else I do to earn a living in order to focus on this project while trying to support my daughter as a single mother. It hasn't been easy.

Having given Mike my word that he would be allowed to remain in total obscurity, I would be forced to accept the brunt of the criticism, and any accusations of falsehood or chicanery would fall squarely on my shoulders. I knew I would have to deal with those who would call me "irresponsible" for publishing a story without a single shred of evidence to back it up.

Would it be worth it? Would the good that could come of publishing the book justify the potentially negative consequences?

I thought again about "trust". I had trusted Mike throughout. I had been a sounding board for him. I had spent literally hundreds of hours with the phone glued to my ear, trying to entertain and care for my 3-year old as I listened to Mike relate his experiences.

Was it wrong to ask for some sort of evidence? He had contacted me, knowing I was a Bigfoot researcher, knowing full well that I would be intrigued by his story. Despite my desire to remain open-minded, any other researcher would have asked for confirmation long before now - and if the witness didn't offer it, they simply would have refused to spend any more of their time on it. Did that make me a "bad researcher"? Or simply more patient?

Initially, he had only wanted to pump me for information. Instead, he ended up with a friend. At least, someone who had tried to be a friend to him, who had done her best to be infinitely patient with his volatile moods and his reluctance to trust... I had been as content as I could be to simply sit back and let him share what he wanted when he wanted, despite the fact that he claimed to hold the knowledge that I'd spent decades searching for.

But despite this, despite all of it, I sit here today, without a bit of evidence that Mike's story is legitimate. Not one photo. Not even a photo of a photo. I have not seen x-rays or medical records or photographs confirming any injuries he claims to have sustained.

I have not seen Shelby's dream-catchers. All I have is myriad explanations for why none of that is available, even privately to me. And his stories, which I cannot discount, no matter how much the inner skeptic wishes me to.

Frankly, I don't know what to do.

Do I throw the book in the trash? Hit delete and forget I ever heard any of it?

The trouble is, I can't. My entire perspective on this subject has been affected by Mike's story. I look at everything differently now. In fact, I have a hard time blogging about Bigfoot on a daily basis, because I feel as if I've leapt light-years ahead in my understanding of this phenomenon – but how can I share that, without context? And how can I share any of it responsibly, knowing that I have absolutely nothing to back it up besides one man's story and my intuition that he is telling the truth?

What about "trust"? I have trusted Mike enough to listen to what he has to say, and believe him. I have trusted him enough to set aside everything else on my plate and focus my full attention on him and his experiences. Mike has trusted me enough to allow me to share his story with you. But his trust goes no further than that.

So I face a difficult decision. I want to follow my heart. I want to write this book the way it was intended to be written: not as exploitation of Mike and Enoch and the relationship they've shared, but as an act of reverence for that relationship; to help Mike share the message that these creatures are not simply cunning animals but are far more beautiful and complex... and deserving of our respect. To hold Mike's unique friendship with Enoch – and mine with Mike - up in a gesture of beauty and respect. A single photograph, a single shred of evidence – while by no means proof - would put it all in perspective and quiet the doubts of those who would question his claims.

And it would finally bring closure to so many, like me, who have caught too short of a glimpse of something that they would like to gaze upon a little longer, in hopes of understanding.

But despite every ounce of energy I have put into this, Mike's final words to me, written on our shared document last weekend, say it all:

"He is my only friend in this world and the only one I can trust, because he don't lie and is always a true friend. That's why he comes first."

Despite the fact that I have never lied to Mike and have been nothing but a friend to him, it doesn't appear to matter in the end. He continues to treat me as a researcher – someone to be mistrusted. It hurts, but there is little I can do about it. I've done all I can. Given the choice of being a researcher or a friend, I will continue to be a friend and I will respect his wishes.

At this point, I don't know what to say - which seems a ridiculous place to be when you're writing the conclusion to a book.

Do I trust Mike? Yes. Do I believe him to be telling the truth? Yes. I find it difficult to believe that anyone could fabricate such an intricate story. But all I have is his word.

And all you have is mine.

And, in the end, I appear to be the only one with something to lose.

We'll have to leave it at that. From what I gather, Mike is going back to the swamp, possibly for good.

In the end, because Mike continues to treat me as a researcher, I am left with no choice but to conclude this as any researcher worth their salt would: I will take it into consideration, and I present it here for your consideration as well. It's all I can do.

Despite the fact that it is a compelling and beautiful story, without evidence, it is simply that.

Another story.

I felt sick, and called Mike. Explaining my predicament, I told him I'd written an ending to the book, but it wasn't the way I wanted to end it.

"You think you're telling me something I don't know? Autumn, I warned you about this a long time ago, and you're just now figuring it out."

"I know," I said, miserably. "I just don't know what to do. I can't go forward. I can't go back."

I felt about an inch tall. After all of this, it was coming down to a lack of trust. No wonder the ending I'd written felt like such a letdown. How could I write a book about trust and have it end like this?

I sent Mike the epilogue and he replied a short time later.

I read this and, to say the least, it stings. To say the most, it's the expected dropping of the other shoe... I am done with Bigfoot people. I want nothing to do with any of this crap ever again. I don't even want to read the rest of the book.

Mike was disgusted with me. I didn't blame him. I was disgusted with myself.

For two weeks, I heard nothing from Mike, and I didn't try to contact him. I sat quietly, at times reflecting so deeply that I was distracted, pulling myself out of my reverie with great effort in order to play with my daughter, be a mom, take care of the house, or speak with doctors as my grandfather's health took a turn for the worse. I couldn't blog, couldn't talk about Bigfoot in a way that anyone would understand anymore, couldn't go back to posting tidbits about Bigfoot sightings and digging into the database to share summaries of hair color and height estimations. Blog readers emailed me from time to time, wondering what was happening with this great revelation I'd had; why I was so quiet.

I was processing; trying to come to terms with what had happened. And wondering just who in the hell I had become.

I remembered what my blog readers had said. "Follow your heart." But try as I might, I couldn't figure out what that meant – what it would *look* like in practice. Or if it was even wise.

Ironically, other events were occurring around this time in my personal life that made this advice even more poignant and significant. Again, it seemed that "coincidences" were converging to a degree that made simple coincidence unimaginable. God, The Cosmos, The Great Mystery or whatever you prefer to call it, deemed it necessary to bring a lesson into my life and was hitting me from all directions at once, swiftly and without mercy. I was hurting. Stung. And deeply humbled. I've always suspected that the presence of irony and coincidence in life are clear indicators that a hard lesson is looming… but the lesson, for the moment, continued to escape me, despite the fact that I was making a conscious effort to *get it*, whatever it was.

Until one morning, when I woke up and it was suddenly, perfectly clear.

Mike was treating me like a researcher because I was acting like one. Again… it was a perfect, beautiful parallel to the Big Guys. They treat us like researchers, and avoid us, because we ACT like researchers.

Someone had said to me recently, "Love abides in the heart… There is no love in the head, it's in the heart."

It dawned on me that I had been "hiding in my head". I'd started out as a witness and had begun researching to try to find answers to what it was that I'd seen, but I had become analytical to a fault. I had become a researcher – and not just a Bigfoot researcher. My desire and readiness to over-analyze things, out of fear of not being able to second-guess an outcome and therefore being out of control, had created turmoil in several of my personal relationships over the years and had nearly destroyed a couple of them – including, now, my friendship with Mike.

Mike's relationship with Enoch was deeply emotional. He experienced Enoch with his heart, not his head. That was what this book was supposed to be about. How, then, could I write it from my head?

This book was not to be a dry relating of facts, backed up by clinically-acquired physical evidence; attempting to prove the existence of Bigfoot; assuaging the potential criticisms of hard-nosed skeptics and researchers with huge expectations and little genuine understanding. Instead, it would be a series of observations and the story of two very delicate friendships: Mike's and Enoch's, and Mike's and mine. It would hopefully relate something deeper and more meaningful than sterile, scientific analysis.

Even if it meant putting myself out there for all of the people who were stuck in their heads to analyze and criticize because I refused to try to pressure Mike into doing something he was uncomfortable with… it was time to follow my heart.

The only thing in my head was *fear*. Fear of, for the first time in my career as a "researcher", *believing* what I knew to be true. Fear of being seen as a "bad researcher". Fear of being ridiculed by other researchers.

Fear of feeling like… *a witness*.

But that's exactly what had started all of this in the first place. Being a witness was the driving force behind all the years I'd spent trying to understand this phenomenon.

I was too much in my head. Following my heart seemed like a good bit of advice, but I perceived a danger there as well. Regardless of how other researchers might feel about me taking off on what might appear to be a completely emotional and subjective tangent, there was my own discomfort with it as well. I didn't want to follow my heart straight off a cliff, so to speak. I didn't want to lose my objectivity. But how to balance the two?

Then it dawned on me.

If you lead with the mind, you risk entrapment in over-analysis and circular thinking. If you follow the heart, it may lead you blindly into a wishfulness that has little to do with reality. But if you listen to your instincts, your intuition, you won't be lead astray. The head thinks. The heart feels. *But the gut knows.*

My gut had been telling me all along that Mike was telling the truth.

And, finally, I knew what I had to do.

-20-

"PROFESSIONAL SUICIDE"

It was Friday, March 5th, 2010. My little girl was asleep in bed and I was putting the last touches on the video editing. I called a friend. "It's going live on Facebook right now. It'll hit the blog in the morning."

Three videos. Three short clips of me talking directly to the camera, addressing the Bigfoot research community, my peers, the critics lying in wait... and the witnesses, who would understand and appreciate what I was about to do.

What follows is a transcript of those videos.

OK... deep breath.

There's a reason that I haven't been blogging very much lately. Um... I'm stuck. I'm kind of in a position that I never wanted to be in, and I really haven't known what to do about it.

When I started out on this journey, I started out as the child of a family of long-term witnesses, which really put me in a position unlike any other. Twenty years ago, when I started doing research, there really weren't any researchers who were witnesses, who had even seen a Sasquatch. And so, coming from where I did, it kind of put me at a disadvantage. And I know that sounds funny, 'A disadvantage.' But it did, because the researchers that I was working with, that I was interacting with, my peers, they didn't know what it felt like to be a witness. And I did. And so I looked at things really differently than most researchers did.

You know, mainstream Bigfoot research has really become something… icky. I don't know how else to say it. There's a, "We take ourselves way too seriously," and a cold objectivity. They want hard facts, details… they believe that makes a good researcher, and in a way they're right, but… the problem is that witnesses are often alienated by that approach and in Bigfoot research – unfortunately, as much as we don't want it to be the case – anecdotal evidence is what we have the most of. I know everybody's running around out there trying to get hard evidence but it's not happening. Why? To truly objectively understand this phenomenon, you have to UNDERSTAND it. Meaning, you have to listen to the people who do, and not just shine them on because they don't bring you an 8 ½ x 11 spiral-bound glossy report with supporting evidence all neatly packaged up, of their encounters. Witnesses are not researchers. And subsequently, researchers are very rarely witnesses. Has that occurred to anybody?

A typical researcher will investigate an incidental witness, an incidental sighting, a road crossing, and they'll sit the witness down and ask them about height and weight and hair color and movement and they want details. More statistical data to add to the database of how they move and what color they are and how tall they might be and how much they weigh. But WHY? What's the point? So you can say you're a researcher and doing something 'researcher-ish'? Are you really getting to the bottom of the mystery? Are you really understanding what these things are? And is that information really helping you in the field aside from… maybe you might know what color of a Sasquatch you hope to run into? (laughs) It just doesn't make any sense. But I understand why this dynamic exists in the research field. Because those are the safe questions. Those are the credible questions. Those are the questions that researchers can ask and the data they can comfortably share with other researchers and then everybody can pat each other on the back and say, "Wow, that's some really good research you did there..." You can call yourself serious and objective and you're not being taken in by a witness who's making grandiose claims. It's easy to believe that someone saw a Bigfoot crossing the road. It's not so easy to believe that they sat down and had a more intimate encounter with them.

Extraordinary claims require extraordinary evidence, right? But what if your witnesses don't want to give you evidence because they don't... like you?

This leaves us in a pickle, because of these high standards that we in the Bigfoot research community hold one another to, because we're worried about the credibility of the field – because there really isn't any. We're a fringe "science". We're left with evidence that does us no good at all. It doesn't prove anything. And it certainly doesn't get us closer to figuring out what these things ARE. Not what they LOOK like, not how they MOVE... but what they ARE. It's a big, big difference.

So then, we take these limited packets of information into the field and this is what we use to determine how we're going to go about our research. And we go out into the woods with our cameras and our high-tech gadgets, creating "Bigfoot ambush", "night-ops" and all this stuff... wearing our camouflage... (laughs) and we miss the point. We completely miss the point, which is that the biggest irony... everybody's trying to be so damned scientific about this... but if you go back and you look at the empirical process, the empirical process states that the whole point of testing a theory is to be able to replicate it. Right? Please explain to me how you're replicating something if a witness tells you that they behaved a certain way [in order to successfully make contact with a Sasquatch] and you go out and behave completely differently? Then you wonder why you don't have any results. Again, let's go back to it: Researchers don't have sightings. Witnesses have sightings – and the reason is that witnesses are NOT researchers. They're not BEHAVING like we are in the field.

Here's a strong statement. Ready for this one? Bigfoot research doesn't work. You want proof of that? We've been chasing our tails for 40 or 50 years, doing the same thing over and over and over again. That's not science. That's stupidity.

But this isn't why I'm stuck. I mean, it kind of is.

The reason that I'm stuck is because several months ago I had a witness come to me with… a story. Boy, is that the understatement of the year. He began opening up to me very tentatively at first… and then more… and over the course of the last few months, I have gotten to a point where I can't blog anymore. I can't do any of the things that any of you expect me to do, because my paradigm has shifted so drastically…

People usually start out in research because they have a curiosity. Just a simple curiosity about this. I had a need. It was a need. I saw something when I was a kid that I didn't understand. I didn't know what the heck it was… and it has shaped the entire course of my life. I eat, breathe, sleep and crap Bigfoot because of it. I became a researcher because I figured that I need to gather information in order to understand what it was that I saw. It was pretty powerful. Otherwise, I wouldn't be doing this. I wouldn't have done it as long as I've done it. I wanted to know what they are. And now I feel like I do.

All of that burning curiosity that I've had for twenty years is satiated. But here's the problem: I know that you have the same questions and I want to share with you the answers that I feel like I've found. But I can't. Can I? Because the answers come from someone who has developed such an intimate relationship with one of these creatures that he sees this creature, this being, as an individual. It's not "a Bigfoot". It's someone he knows. And he's very protective and he doesn't want to exploit him and I don't blame him. But then that leaves me in a pickle because acting as a researcher I can't hold a gun to the guy's head and say, "Ok, that's great, you shared your story with me, now give me proof." Because he doesn't want to. He doesn't want to have a picture of this guy slathered all over the internet and ripped off and put up on every Bigfoot website. It's exploitive. And he doesn't like Bigfoot researchers. He said to me one time that letting a Bigfoot researcher into where he is would be like letting a pedophile loose in a daycare when your kid's there. And I don't think I've ever heard it put more succinctly. I understand exactly how he feels. So I have all of this information, these detailed observations that he's shared with me and he's willing to let me share with you. But I can provide no proof. And I know exactly what's going to happen if I do it. Every Bigfoot researcher, the whole peanut gallery, is going to say, "If you can't provide any evidence then what good does this do any of us?" Because of those standards. Because of those narrow standards that have had us not just barking up the wrong tree... we're not even in the forest anymore and that, sir, is not a tree. That's a telephone pole.

It's just gotten ridiculous.

So here is a witness who is sharing information that any [researcher] worth their salt can hear and know that it makes sense. This is a very unique situation. There was a perfect storm of events that created it.

But can I share it? Can I share with you what's been shared with me?
The answer is, yes. I can.

I've been agonizing over this because I've spent 20 years in this field being careful, minding my Ps and Qs, toeing the party line, building credibility. For what? So that when I finally feel like the answers have landed in my lap, I can't share them with you?

Bullshit.

I slept on this the other night and I woke up and I realized… it hit me. I have never been a Bigfoot researcher first. I was a witness. And throughout 20 years of doing this, my main focus has always been eyewitness confidentiality, the safety of these creatures that we're studying… and being there for eyewitnesses to have someone to listen to them.

I am not a Bigfoot researcher. I'm an eyewitness advocate. And there is a huge difference.

Because of that, I'm officially hanging up my Bigfoot researcher hat. Throwing in the towel. Handing back the title. You guys can keep on doing what you've been doing for 40 or 50 years. Go ahead. You want to prove it? You think you can prove it? Be my guest. It'll mean the demise of the species – but if that's what you think you need to do, go ahead. I don't have any interest in proving this. I know that these things exist and every single witness out there, every person who's seen one of these, THEY know that they exist. So this isn't a matter [to them or me] of, "Hey, let's prove it..."

Prove it to whom? To the people who don't believe it? They've got their reasons for not believing it. They're not going to believe it anyways. Prove it to science? Why? So they can be dissected? Prove it so we can "protect them"? That's the most asinine thing I've ever heard. The only people that these things need protecting from is Bigfoot researchers who go out there and bang on trees and harass them. Think about that. Why would we need to protect Sasquatch from science? They're not paying any attention. We don't need to protect them from the government. They're not paying any attention. Or, if they are, we don't know about it. Who are we going to protect them from except us? They don't need protection.

I'm three-quarters of the way through the book. And I'm releasing this in book format because this story and the message deserves full context. Because it is more complex and more intricate and more involved than anything I've ever come across as a researcher. I'm going to publish this book, not for researchers, but for witnesses. If you accept the story, the anecdotal evidence, the same way you accept that someone saw a Bigfoot cross the road, by the time you're done reading the book, you're going to be in the same boat that I am. And I think you'll have a lot of questions answered. And I think you'll understand, too, that being a researcher doesn't mean that we don't have a moral and an ethical responsibility to both the creatures that we're researching and the witnesses who are sharing their information with us.

Think about Jane Goodall. Jane Goodall started out as a chimp researcher and what is she now? She's a conservationist. Dian

Fossey? Same deal. People start out as researchers and they become conservationists because they learn to care about what it is they're researching. Because they learn about it. Really learn about it. The trouble with us? We haven't learned anything. What do we know? What do we really know about Bigfoot as Bigfoot researchers? What do we really know?

"Bigfoot researcher"? That doesn't even mean anything anymore. Do you want to know what it means? It means that when some new guy comes into this field, he goes around on the internet and he sees all these websites of all these other guys with the high-tech gadgetry and he sees all the YouTube videos of all these people banging on trees and knocking on wood and making all these sounds and… scaring off all the wildlife. (laughs) And he thinks, "Wow. That looks cool. I wanna do that!"
And, hey, the title's free, right? Read a couple of books, develop an interest and all of a sudden you're a Bigfoot researcher.

Well, I'm not.

Not anymore.

 I sent Mike a link to the blog the next day and waited. We hadn't spoken in a couple of weeks, but I had a feeling I'd be hearing from him any minute now.
 It wasn't long before my email notification chimed.

Subject: What have you been smoking?

What the hell… I log on this morning and find your email, listened to your blog, sat back and thought about it for a minute and have come to wonder…

Have you lost your mind, fell head first off the cabbage wagon, been smoking wacky weed, or did you finally get it? Did the light come on and you understand what I have been trying to tell you? What you are doing will do more to make them understand than if you gave them a dead body, do you understand that? Proof ain't nothing without understanding. I don't want to prove it to them. I can do that all day. I want them to take the leap and believe it with their hearts.

That is why I believe the book will make more of an impact without proof. I want them and you to read it and understand why I feel the way I do.

I want them to read and reread it, study it like they would a history book, read between the lines and go with Enoch and I on our journey to understanding each other... and that includes you too.

I don't know what's in store for us. Only time will tell. I am glad you have learned you don't have to go with the herd and have started a new and better trail.

If you follow too close to the horse in front of you, all you see is a horse's ass. But if you go your own way...

Smell ya later, Autumn Gator.

Mike

> The subsequent backlash was mostly predictable:
> "She's trying to drum up interest in her book..."
> "She's being taken for a ride..."
> "She should seek mental health counseling..."

"She's a drama queen..."

"Why is she pretending there's such a void between witnesses and researchers?"

Once again, I was struck by the irony. Those who were getting offended by the things I said in my video blog in regards to the way research is being conducted and how witnesses are being treated, and making it *apparent* that they found it offensive, were pinpointing themselves as the very ones I was directing my comments to. Unwittingly, as they publicly decried the criticisms and made it clear how threatened they felt by the things I'd said, they raised their hands and identified themselves as the very subject of those criticisms!

Those who hold strong beliefs about what Bigfoot is, and is not, are easily upset when someone tips the apple cart. Or even *mentions* tipping it. The strangest part about it was that I hadn't even told them WHAT I was going to say. Just that I was going to say something that they may not want to hear.

For these folks, proof probably *is* necessary. It's difficult to change a belief system without it.

But the strange reactions didn't stop there. One blogger went so far as to state, in his "professional opinion", that my tongue-in-cheek mention of professional suicide was an actual call for help and that my peers in the research community shouldn't be angry with me for taking our methods to task because I had much bigger mental health issues and was obviously literally suicidal... A post which darkly underscored the tabloid sensationalism that I've come to expect from the mass media, but which was more disturbing coming from someone who is generally revered as "one of us" in the Cryptozoology field. (I wondered how my daughter would have felt if she'd stumbled upon that particular piece of unfounded gossip - that her mother was supposedly suicidal – had she been old enough to read and comprehend it.)

The number of disagreeing yet respectful responses that were posted on public forums by researchers surprised me. "I don't agree with Autumn, but I respect her right to follow the path she sees fit." Having been a part of the research community for so many years – and at the mercy of it a time or two - I honestly hadn't expected that degree of equanimity from my peers. I had made many, many friends in the research community over the years, and I wondered: was the perceived "majority" of the potential detractors in the research community really a minority, or had the friendships and alliances I'd made over the years created a support system that would allow me to go out on a limb?

The support from blog readers, who are primarily witnesses and Bigfoot enthusiasts, was overwhelming. They didn't care for proof; they simply wanted to read the information and make up their own minds about it.

I knew that the witnesses would likely get the most out of this book. The information Mike shared with me had provided comfort and some sort of closure about what I'd seen... the "witness" in me resonated with Mike's perspective as a witness, and I wanted to share that with others. Felt compelled to, in fact. Not only to get it off my chest, but because seeing a Sasquatch can leave a lasting impression and have a powerful, sometimes devastating effect on a witness' life and there can be comfort in knowing that you're not alone.

I received the following email about three weeks after posting the video blog:

I am a former Natural Resources teacher and professional Habitat Restoration field biologist... that is until I went public [about my Bigfoot sightings] with my friends and peers at a new job (Executive Director for a non-profit dedicated to protecting habitat for native fish)... then I suddenly lost my job, with no explanation and have been unemployed for 26 months now... some kind of professional outcast it seems.

And so, when I watched your video blog about Professional Suicide, I thought that it might be about environmental professionals who are afraid to come forward and go through what I am going through now...

I used to think that seeing what I've seen and experiencing what I've experienced was a blessing, but lately, I've felt that it is more of a curse. Every year at about this season, I have dreams of seeing BF again and escaping to the forests near Mt. Rainier to surround myself with trees, by myself with no one else around... the only time that I truly feel at peace... but then again at times terrified that I will come face to face with another massive giant of the Pacific NW... I was close enough to see an ear and realize that it looked just like on the side of a gorilla's head. And while it was crossing the pavement in front of me... I did slam on my breaks, stalling my car and almost running after it into the darkness... only to come back the next day and find the tree bough it pushed out of its face was about 10 feet off the ground... at chin level... I followed actual physical evidence through deep needle duff (scuff marks) for over 100 yards until they went over the edge of a steep embankment and left deep imprints in the hill side as it walked down hill on two legs and into another, yet darker stand of trees...

I've always figured that the reason that I've had four encounters at various ages is that these individuals and I tend to share the same habitat from time to time... as I love to be outdoors... hiking, camping, fishing, (formerly hunting), mushroom and berry picking, etc. I just happen to like to be in places where the creatures live... I don't really go out looking for them, however I do return to my old haunts from time to time... just to look for fresh tracks near the waterways, as I would give anything to just one last time, meet one... but this time face to face... just long enough to briefly look each other in the eye... nod in respect and acknowledging each others existence and say, "I see you grandfather... go in peace."

Thank you again for your touching video clips... it gave me a chance to see the real you... for you see, I'm not a real fan of BF "researchers" as a whole, myself and I thought that you were one of "them"... and now I know that you and I are both one of "us"... the witnesses.

PS... I truly do hope to meet you someday and share a cup of your favorite beverage and swap stories about our experiences... with another witness... (damn... I can't believe that my eyes started watering... got a little emotional about wanting another person to just talk to who can understand what I've seen and felt all these years... feel kind of stupid... felt like crying for a second when I thought about actually meeting someone who might actually understand and not think I was completely nuts... as my entire family does... the emotion just really caught me off guard... weird.)

    Speaking to this man on the phone, he mentioned again how he was moved by the video blogs. As a witness, my feelings of frustration spoke to him.

On the other hand, many researchers accused me of being "emotionally overwrought" or "dramatic" or "insincere" - all in an attempt to sell books.

My frustration in those blogs stemmed from speaking as a witness. Not a researcher. It resonated with other witnesses. The fact that many researchers didn't interpret the emotion behind my words properly wasn't surprising.

But there is supposedly no void of understanding between witnesses and researchers.

-21-

WHAT IS A SASQUATCH?

As you've read this book, you may have picked up quite a few new ideas, or felt as if something you've suspected about these creatures is confirmed in some way. On the other hand, if you hold steadfast beliefs or opinions about what Bigfoot is or is not, you may be experiencing irritation, incredulity or even anger with Mike or me by now.

This isn't the whole story. To share the volumes of information with you that Mike has shared with me, it would take an encyclopedia-sized set of books. The small details he has mentioned in passing that seem insignificant to him have helped to put these creatures into such a context for me that I can only scratch the surface of it here. And Mike continually reminds me that he has left things out as well, both intentionally and unintentionally. How does one begin to explain to another the things they've come to realize through personal experience? Mike has been trying for months to share with me years' worth of interactions, and has reminded me repeatedly that he's likely forgotten more than he's related. Similarly, how do I share with you the hundreds of hours of conversations, the subtle nuances in Mike's voice as he relates a story, the emotion I feel and that I hear from him, the sometimes seemingly innocuous questions I ask that lead to profound comprehension?

Along the way, those subtleties have filled in the blanks in regards to my understanding. It's not that we didn't have the pieces of the puzzle all along. We just didn't know where they fit. It's not that we've been all *wrong* all along about the Sasquatch. The small clarities necessary to truly empathize and know how best to interact with them have simply been lost somewhere in the assumptions we've made.

So what is a Sasquatch?

The answer I feel comfortable with at this point is so complex, yet so simple, that it's difficult to know where to begin.

Are they human or animal?

First, please allow me to clarify, because I've concluded that two individuals asking this question be seeking two very different answers.

Are we referring to their genetic makeup? Or simply their nature?

Some very literally want to know: are they *Homo Sapiens* – in other words, are they genetically identical to us? Or something else entirely? Where do they lie on the evolutionary "bush"? Are they a "missing link"? Our genetic ancestor? Or something far removed?

While this question might be answered by acquiring a specimen, I personally don't wish for an answer so fervently that I would condone sacrificing one of their kind in order to assuage my curiosity and damn the consequences, both to the individual Sasquatch who sacrifices its life and to the species as a whole when the discovery is made. Does the end always justify the means? I don't believe so. Unfortunately, I imagine there are those who don't have a moral or ethical dilemma when it comes to "scientific advancement" or the pursuit of knowledge.

Personally, when I ponder where they fall in the realm of human and animal, I am referring to their *nature* and how they conduct themselves. Their intelligence level. The way they socialize. These questions can and should be answered without a corpse – and are, in fact, better addressed through observation of living subjects than a body on a table.

Thanks to Mike, I feel that this question has been answered somewhat to my satisfaction; but in order to explain the context in which the answer has come, I'm afraid I have to digress.

After Mike agreed to let me include his story in this book, he called me one day and said, "I don't like the term Skunk Ape. Or Bigfoot. I want you to change it." Many things Mike said during our conversations initially felt as if they came out of left field and this was no different. But I took it in stride.

"Why?" I asked.

"Well, I referred to him as a Skunk Ape in there because that's what they call them down here. But I don't like it. I never have. It's disrespectful… and it's not accurate. I mean, he smells bad sometimes, but…"

I understood. That's not what made Enoch… *Enoch*. He wasn't a skunk… and he wasn't an ape. He wasn't simply a big, smelly, two-legged gorilla and Mike felt it was wrong to refer to him as such. Again, it went back to the fact that Mike saw this individual as a friend. Calling him names felt wrong to him.

"Can you come up with something more accurate?" I asked. "Is there a term or a label you can apply to all of them that would be more suitable, and that would encompass their nature and help communicate what they are?"

"I don't know," Mike replied. "I'll have to think about it."

And he did. But he was unable to come up with anything that was short and to-the-point. "It's like this," he stressed again, as we discussed it further. "If you took a human child and left him out in the woods, then came back in 10 or 15 years, what would you find? A wild human. Still human. But wild. That's what these guys are like."

A Wild Man.

The distinction, I would come to find, was subtle. But important. The full extent of it didn't hit me until a week before I was due to write the final chapter of this book.

They live and survive like animals, but they socialize much like primitive humans.

Bigfoot, Sasquatches, Skunk Apes, Wild Men... they don't depend upon the things that humans do for their survival: Fire, tools, permanent shelter, transportation, clothing... They are not concerned with artifacts or artifice. Unlike us, they are supremely suited to living in their environment. They live very differently than we do and therefore it is difficult, as dependent as we are upon the things we create for consistency and convenience, to truly comprehend that.

When I asked Mike whether they appeared to value possessions, he replied, "I've seen them use things they've found. Like, if someone leaves a towel on the riverbank, a momma will wrap her baby up in it. I've seen them carry water in an old cooler." But he made it clear to me that they do not appear to take these things with them if they leave. Found objects are used for the sake of convenience. When asked if they use tools, Mike said, "I've seen them carrying clubs. They'll strip the branches off a limb and use it to whack a hog in the head." Beyond this, it doesn't appear that they will modify an object in any complex way to serve a specific purpose. They simply will use found or handy objects; discarding them when they're no longer needed. It makes sense: the reason something becomes a *possession*, and someone becomes possessive of that thing, is because an investment of time and care was put into creating or obtaining the object for a particular purpose, intends to use it again, and doesn't want to go to the time and expense of re-creating it. If you make use of what's at hand, you have no need to carry a backpack full of items that serve a specific purpose... or have a house in which to store and protect them.

Their survival, ultimately, depends upon staying as far away from humans as possible except in rare circumstances. And they're suited for that, as well. They leave little trace, they forage on the go, they appear to be both nomadic and territorial, and their ability to move isn't bogged down by armloads of possessions. In other words, you'll never see a Wild Man with a U-Haul.

Survival, to them, is key – and the things they do *deliberately* ensure it. If you're curious what a Bigfoot would do in any given situation, simply ask yourself: "What would I do in order to best ensure *my* survival in that situation?"

This was illustrated many times in Mike's discussions with me and it soon became apparent that it was a constant underlying concern.

Researchers often ponder whether Sasquatches are territorial or nomadic. Because long-term witnesses have inevitably mentioned that the creatures only appear to be around during certain seasons, I've always suspected that they're both. They are nomadic in the sense that they move seasonally, due to climate (comfort) concerns and food resources. But the areas in which they move to are specific territories with which they are familiar. It's always made sense to me that they would not simply wander aimlessly, but would go to a known area in which food is available and humans are scarce. There would be no reason for the creatures to wander into unknown territory, risking a lack of food and privacy, when there is a known area that provides for their survival.

Mike's observations tend to support this and he has said numerous times, "I hardly ever see him in the summer. The mosquitoes are real bad that time of year – they'll eat you alive. He always seems to be around in the fall and winter." Because he's noticed a pattern in the seasons in which Enoch is present over the years, Mike has surmised that he travels somewhere else when the heat and the mosquitoes become unbearable. He also mentioned, recently, that Shelby had "returned" after being absent for a long time. She appeared exhausted and the bottoms of her feet were "torn up", as if she had traveled a considerable distance.

That Mike observed a group of them for some time supports another suspicion of mine: that they travel in small, independent family groups, but meet up at particular destinations. It would be illogical – again, for the sake of survival – for the creatures to move in large groups from one destination to another. The evidence of their passing would amount to that of a herd of elephants, and remaining elusive while traveling in a large group would be difficult. But neither would it follow that small units of Sasquatches would wander aimlessly, bumping into one another only serendipitously; especially when they appear to be social creatures (a matter we'll address shortly). At the rendezvous, after the juvenile died and was buried, Mike observed the creatures dispersing from the gathering in small family units over a period of several days. While he directly observed nothing that would suggest that they were all headed off to meet up at another location later, it's implausible to assume that the gathering he observed was the only one that has ever taken place.

The other reason that I suspect the gatherings occur more often than we might suspect is because of the social interactions Mike has witnessed.

The rendezvous occurred in a location that ensured little or no human discovery. Remember, at one point Mike was forced to wade through neck-deep water in an environment in which leeches, alligators and poisonous snakes were a real threat. When he arrived at the rendezvous, it was only by the grace of Enoch's ambassadorship that his presence was tolerated – and then only at the fringe.

But what Mike observed during those weeks appeared to be a *social* gathering. He has discussed the details of this with me many times, and it is through these multiple, detailed descriptions that I have come to realize that these creatures *socialize like humans*, despite the fact that they survive like animals. And therein lays the distinction. They do not behave like apes.

"They don't sit with their backs to each other, like a bunch of gorillas. It was more like a family picnic or a reunion or something. Each little family group wallowed out a cubby in the brush and that was their space. But then the little ones would come out play together in the clearing, while the women looked on. The females all sat together and jabbered and gestured – it reminded me of my Grandma's sewing circle."

Mike has mentioned several times how the creatures gesture and "talk". He has even mentioned that there appears to be humor in their interactions: that one will say something, and another will jabber back and whack the other on the arm.

At one point, shortly after Mike first arrived at the rendezvous, two of the males appeared to be discussing him. "They were talking to each other and gesturing. One of them kept looking over at me while they were talking and I could tell that they were *discussing* me. I think they were deciding what to do about me being there."

He has also observed a young male "discouraged" from approaching a young female. The older male, presumably her father, vocalized and gestured angrily.

While it could be argued that the creatures are simply making nonsensical sounds that do not constitute a "language", Mike's reluctance to over-interpret what he's witnessed and his adamancy that the creatures are communicating clearly with one another through spoken words leads me to think otherwise. When primates interact with one another, they tend to make sounds based upon specific, immediate events. For instance, one chimpanzee will approach another who has food in its possession, and there will be a cacophony of screeching and displays of aggression. However, Mike has shared numerous occasions in which he's witnessed quiet, deliberate conversations, the context of which was nearly understandable to him. He likens it to listening to his Spanish-speaking co-workers. He cannot speak Spanish, but he's usually able to comprehend the essence of the conversation, whether by tone, inflection, body language… or simply because he's heard the language often enough that he's beginning to experience literal subconscious language comprehension.

Observing these creatures sharing food is another social behavior that Mike has related many times, and it supports the idea that survival is a priority. It seems to me that in our increasing tendency toward consumption and self-absorption, survival of the individual, and not the group, is another thing that separates us from truly understanding these creatures.

Mike began giving Enoch food in his camp, and suspected that there were others nearby when Enoch would take copious amounts with him when he left. At the rendezvous, his suspicions were confirmed. Mike observed males bringing in full deer carcasses. They would tear off a hindquarter and leave it at their family "cubby", then toss the rest of the carcass in the clearing, where the others would come and take what they wanted from it. Enoch would bring Mike dead animals. Not wanting to eat them, but not wanting to be rude, he would cook the offerings and leave them in the clearing, and the group would take what they wanted. According to Mike, as the rapport between he and Enoch grew from the beginning, so did Enoch's willingness to *share with Mike* rather than seeing him as simply a source of food.

I suspect that this information could be useful to long-term witnesses in gauging the success of their rapport-building endeavors with the Big Guys. For instance, if you leave out a large box of apples and the entire box is taken, you're still on the outside looking in. If only half of the apples are taken, you're almost there. But once the Big Guy comes and sits down at the box, grabs an apple, pops it in his mouth and also tosses you one, you're in. You've been accepted. If you're important enough to share food with, they care enough about you to ensure your survival, too.

Mike's observations have included details about the creatures' varying appearances as well. He has often described at least two different "flavors" of the creature, as he puts it. Some are more human looking, and some appear more gorilla-like. (Interestingly, this addresses one of the conundrums I've always faced regarding eyewitnesses describing these creatures in varying degrees of "human-like" or "gorilla-like" I've wondered whether it was a function of the witness' particular interpretation, or an actual difference in appearance.) Describing the gorilla-like ones, Mike makes it clear that their facial features do not resemble those of a gorilla. The nose is not squashed with large nostrils, and the mouth area does not protrude. What makes them appear gorilla-like is that they are bulkier, have darker complexions, and the hair on the face is slightly different – not so much like a human beard. But he makes it clear, as well, that some of them seem to be almost a combination of both. Enoch, for instance, has a darker complexion, but has human-like facial hair. "The human-looking ones really do look like a bunch of long-haired hippies…"

He also mentioned that the more gorilla-looking creatures tend to be more aggressive and often take the role of "sentry". He stated that, when he would be escorted back to his camp, it was usually by two of the gorilla-looking males. He didn't notice any particular difference in intelligence or language ability between the two types – only a difference in appearance and seeming "standoffishness" – the darker-complexioned, bulkier creatures being the more elusive of the two.

Interestingly, Mike pointed out that, at the rendezvous, the human-looking and gorilla-looking creatures tended to separate into cliques. "It's not that they didn't interact, but if two of the females who looked more human were sitting together, the gorilla-looking females wouldn't join them." He likened it to watching different ethnicities naturally congregate into cliques during lunchtime at work.

Mike never tried to explain or interpret the differences in appearance, aside from saying, "They're just like people. They all have different facial features, different body shapes, different hair colors…"

Juveniles appear to grow quickly. "A young one that seems to be 7 years of age or so [in Mike's rough estimation of age based appearance and emotional maturity] can be 6 feet tall."

The males were bolder, more likely to bring mischief. The young females seemed more prone to compassion and affection and tended to hang back as the boys harassed him.

Mike and I discussed the numerous reports in my files of campers being terrified by creatures whooping, hollering, throwing rocks and sticks and the like. In many instances, Mike suspects, those campers were at the mercy not of angry, territorial adult Sasquatches but of wild juvenile delinquents who were simply playing games and trying to get a reaction out of the weird little hairless people in the woods. Testing boundaries. Learning through cause and effect. It's what kids do.

Mike mentioned that the juveniles all played together, and that they tended to respond *immediately* when summoned by an adult. (I'm sure that many parents, like me, would like to know just how exactly they manage to succeed at getting the youngsters to listen so well…) Young Sasquatches likely face many more dangers on a daily basis than human children do. Again, one would assume that this would be taught at an early age as a function of survival.

Like human children, however, the juveniles appear to be equally unconcerned with survival from a conscious standpoint. From Mike's descriptions, they tend to act rather like our own children – playing games in order to learn about the world, testing boundaries, experimenting, knocking the hats off unsuspecting humans who venture too far into their backyard...

Adult Sasquatches, according to Mike's observations, tend to be more sober, cautious, preoccupied with survival and care of children and much less free-spirited; kind of like adult humans. It's really not much of a stretch: I worry about how I'm going to pay the power bill, fix the toilet and keep my child from killing herself while she pulls the cat's tail and promptly turns and chases a butterfly into the street. A wild mother in the swamp gathers food and teaches her child about the danger of water moccasins as he climbs a tree and tries to break his neck.

I feel her pain.

Repeatedly, Mike made a comment to me that stuck. "If a Skunk Ape sees you, you don't belong to your momma no more. You belong to him." He reiterated that these creatures do what they want, when they want to. Several of his encounters with Enoch ended in Mike getting hurt, because he did something, apparently, that Enoch didn't like; something that threatened his survival. Enoch's knee-jerk reactions are a survival mechanism as well. Unlike humans, who are taught from a young age not to hit, to "use words", to talk things out, to suppress our baser instincts in most cases from behaving aggressively when someone does something we don't like, Enoch and his kind apparently are taught just the opposite. Immediately mitigate the threat.

Many researchers claim that Sasquatches in certain areas are more aggressive than in others. Are they? Or are the researchers themselves contributing to situational aggression with their behavior?

I suspect that many cases in which Sasquatch are perceived as acting "aggressively" (in other words, as if they're some sort of dangerous wild animal) are not actually aggression at all. It's simply us getting in the way of a Bigfoot and what he wants, or is comfortable with.

On a recent blog, an eyewitness reported that he sustained injuries when a creature tossed him off an embankment. It proceeded to help itself to the man's lunch on the tailgate of his pickup. I don't think the creature was being genuinely hostile. He just wanted what he wanted and the witness was in the way. Nevertheless, blog readers posted comments crying for blood, like an angry mob with torches and pitchforks. Perceiving aggression where there is none can be dangerous – both for them, and us. Before we know it, truckloads of yahoos with guns and a misguided sense of anger are out chasing the "monster" – who simply wanted a sandwich.

However, Mike has cautioned me repeatedly to be careful how I conduct myself in the woods, and not to simply assume that these creatures mean no harm in all cases. "Again... they're like people. Some of them are kind. Some of them are assholes." I've learned from Mike's encounters that it's not a good idea to irritate a Skunk Ape, to take away their feeling of control over the situation. Trouble is, it's difficult to know precisely what constitutes a "mistake" until you make it.

Mike's advice: Shining a light in their eyes or trying to film them is a big no-no. Ironically, that seems to be what people want to do most often.

My perspective on Bigfoot research has changed dramatically. Lately, I've come to realize that it has been our *lack of understanding of what is possible* that has caused us to spend so many years chasing our tails.

The other day, I was on the phone with a researcher friend of mine. He consistently expressed a desire to record more vocalizations at a distance or be "lucky" enough to capture Bigfoot's image on a game camera. These have been the common goals of most researchers – myself included, in the past. What we've failed to realize is that there are experiences waiting for us far beyond a brief glimpse, a blurry photo, or an inconclusive audio recording.

I asked him the same question I'd asked another researcher friend last year. "Do you want to prove it to the world? Or do you want to have the experience of a lifetime?"

He answered, "I'd want to experience it, I guess."

"But what if," I said, "experiencing it meant that you would come to care about them so deeply that you wouldn't *want* prove it, even though you'd be in the perfect position to do so, because doing so would feel like exploitation?"

He was quiet.

"That's the secret," I told him. "The more you witness, the less you feel the need to research. *And the more you research, the less you'll witness.*"

"But if I just keep doing what I'm doing, I might get lucky," he insisted.

"I guess it depends on what you consider 'luck'. Who's luckier... the guy who is convinced that he can trick a Sasquatch and spends his life trying to get a photo on a game camera? Or the one who is able to sit there with him for hours... and hand him an apple... because he put the cameras away and focused on trust?"

"But you can't even *see* my game camera on the tree, it's so well-camouflaged. It's even got real bark on it."

"Right." I said gently. "He probably won't notice your camera on that tree that he's passed by hundreds of times. He probably won't associate *you* with that strange thing, either, even though he watched you from the woods while you were putting it up."

My goals have changed.

There was a time when I would have been grateful for a glimpse of a large, hairy creature running from me, a pristine line of tracks, a crystal-clear audio recording, a photo of a Bigfoot caught unawares on a game camera. Now, because of what Mike has shared with me, I approach my time in the woods very differently.

There have been several independent reports in my area of an elderly, grey-bearded Sasquatch who limps. Recently, he was spotted digging through trashcans at a park, presumably looking for food.

I felt sick when I heard that several would-be researchers, new to the chase, were putting up cameras in the area. As if he doesn't have enough to worry about already.

I hiked into a draw last weekend with a basket of food. Apples, raisins, a loaf of bread, grapes, and a Little Debbie snack cake. And no camera. I didn't want anything from him. I just wanted to help him out.

In your mind, Mike's story may be just that. A story. But the value in it, whether you believe it to be true or not, is that it just might cause you to think outside the box; to reexamine your goals. If your goal is simply to photograph a Bigfoot on a game camera and everything you do is toward that end… Who knows? In the end, maybe you'll get lucky. And when you've accomplished your goal, what will you have? A photo on a game camera. But what if you apply the same energy and patience toward seeking interaction and you are equally successful? You just might have the experience of a lifetime.

There is a downside.

Mike had kept his secret for ten years before sharing his story with me. "I couldn't tell anybody. The one person I showed the photos to double-crossed me. So every time I took off for the swamp, I had to make excuses about where I'd been and what I was doing. My siblings thought I was gone on jobs. Nobody in my life knows anything about this. It's like I'm living two lives. I can't talk about it at work, even when the other guys are standing around on break talking about Skunk Apes. I have to pretend I don't know anything.

"No one knows about my friendship with you. I can't tell anybody that we're friends. And now that you're writing this book, I can't tell anybody about that either. It's just one damned secret after another."

* * * * *

There are probably dozens of other subjects that I should cover here that Mike has touched on in one way or another. Every time we talk, I feel I learn something new. But now that all of this is off my chest and there is a fully-contextual frame of reference that I can point people to in order to explain *why* I now think about this subject the way I do, I plan to continue exploring these ideas within the Oregon Bigfoot blog[1] as they come up.

What's next? For now, I'll keep on spending time in the woods with my daughter. Someday, I'd like to purchase a small piece of property with a cabin on it, perhaps on the

---

[1] http://www.oregonbigfoot.com/blog/

edge of a National Forest. Preferably one that is being sold cheaply, because the current occupants are tired of dealing with big, hairy, creepy people stomping around their house in the middle of the night. When that day finally comes, I will plant a garden, grow some fruit trees, share the spoils and hope to develop a lasting friendship with our barefoot neighbors in the woods.

-22-

FINAL THOUGHTS

I asked Mike if there was anything he'd like to say – any final thoughts he'd like to share with those of you who have chosen to accompany us on this journey. This is what he wrote:

I wanted to say a few things to all of you who have stood with Autumn through all of this.

I want you to know that I appreciate all the kind words and support you have given her. She has been through hell and back trying to put this book together, and as she found out I can be hard to deal with and that I stand strong in my convictions. The safety of my friend comes first. I will not do anything to put him in harm's way, and I will not be pushed into something that I feel is not in his or my best interest.

I would not have let Autumn put herself in the line of fire unless I could back up my claims with hard proof. That being said, when and if I feel the time is right and I know that no harm will come to him, only then will I provide proof.

My dislike for Bigfoot researchers is no front-page news. I say to you: choose your words carefully, because in time I may decide to make you eat them. But I'll tell you what... you show me the clear, close-up pictures of bigfoot on your camera, and I'll show you mine.

I chose Autumn for a very good reason: Because she gets it. She understands what she is dealing with and her heart is in the right place. Bigfoot research has never worked in the first place and it is pointless to pursue that kind of so-called "research".

I think it will be people like Autumn and other witnesses who will be on the front lines of Bigfoot research, not knocking on trees but sitting still and letting Bigfoot find them. The few lucky ones who Bigfoot has already found know the truth - and that, in my mind, is all that really matters in the end. You are the ones who already know that Bigfoot is alive and well. This book is for you to read and enjoy and I hope it helps you understand them a little better.

This is a true story: not about finding Bigfoot, but about finding what's in your heart and building friendship and trust. It will have tested what you think you know and believe about the Big Guys... and yourself.

I didn't want to share any proof with the book. I want you to believe. To understand. Not to look at a picture of my friend and know what he looks like, but to open your heart and mind. To take that leap toward understanding them as they are.

Here's a Bigfoot fact for you: a body on a slab or a photo will not tell you who they are. It will only tell you what we've become. That is not where the answers are. The answers lie in getting to know them and interacting with them.

To do this, you must stop chasing them and give them a reason to trust you. That is the key. Researchers don't understand this and never will. That's why they fail over and over again. They think they are smarter than what they chase. They underestimate the Big Guys and are easily fooled.

For me, it took learning to look through the eyes of my friend and opening my mind to understand what he is and who I am.
I looked deep inside myself and didn't like what I saw; but with his friendship and trust, I was able to come back from the brink.

I wanted to give you a small look through the window to their world, a small glimpse into their lives and the way they live, in hopes that you can see the world through their eyes.

The meaning of the book and its message will be lost on those who refuse to open their minds and their hearts, and are not willing to make the leap it takes to understand.

I am forever grateful to Autumn for making this happen. The Big Guys, me, and you, the witness, could not have a better friend than her.

Smell ya later...

Mike

Having never written a book before, it's difficult to know when it's "finished"; especially when the story - both Mike's and Enoch's and Mike's and mine - is ongoing.

I have shared what I can of this profound and personal journey. There are many things Mike has asked me not to include. There are probably some points I would have liked to have made that I haven't, or ideas that I'd like to share that were simply too complex to put into words right now. This is a learning process, and I'm still learning. I'm sure that my understanding will continue to evolve long after this book is published; Mike has a great deal more to share and teach me if he is willing. In fact, *he's* still learning. There are many things he's alluded to, as usual, the details of which I still haven't heard. I don't know that I ever will. I know that depends upon whether our friendship continues to grow or he decides to fade back into the swamp.

I've been asked whether I plan to visit Mike. Yes. We're making plans for me to visit him in the fall, or perhaps next spring. There have been circumstances that have prevented my hopping on a plane in the last few months: financial constraints, finding someone to watch my daughter while I'm gone... not to mention my fear of flying. There are those who will question whether I "should" have gone to visit him before the book was published, to "verify" his story. It may be difficult to understand that I feel no need to do so. Mike, the witness, speaks to the witness in me and my gut tells me all I need to know.

When I finally do accompany Mike into the swamp, it will not be to confirm his claims, or to document whatever occurs there. I will step off the plane, hug my friend, get on the boat, enjoy his company, share a few laughs, revel in the wild beauty, camp on a sandbar, trust that his knowledge of the swamp will protect me from any dangers there... and I will sit quietly with empty hands and an open heart if Enoch pays us a visit.

I will feel awe I'm sure. Wonder. I may extend a hand in friendship. But I will not have a camera in the other.

I won't bring back souvenirs from Bigfootland. The only thing I will leave with is the memories of any experiences I have while I am there.

For me, that is enough.

* * * * *

SUNDAY 02/28/2010

Shelby's back. Two hips and a hooray! I'm so glad to see her. She has grown into a lovely young lady.

Cora Beth is back also… with her mate. Now I have to find out where Enoch fits in with all this. I wonder if there was some swamp ape hanky-panky going on when he brought her to camp before.

Shelby stayed in camp all night. She curled up on my sleeping bag and slept most of the night. She looks tired; as if she traveled a long way to get here.

I am going to town to get her something special today. Also, I'm running out of food. Damn, they eat a lot. $300 in two days.

Last night was better than ever. I went to their camp and it was full of Big Guys and Gals. I counted twelve adults and six little ones.

Not including Shelby… she is in a class by herself. It was a big weight lifted off my shoulders to see her and to know that she is all right.

It was funny: I was walking through the woods on my way to their camp when someone ran up behind me and took my hat and ran off with it. A short time later, someone came up from behind me, grabbed my pack and pulled me backward until I fell down.

I was on my back and saw this face looking down at me, upside down. We were nose to nose, and then she put her cheek next to mine.

I said, "Hello, Shelby. I'm so glad to see you! Did you miss me?"

She let me sit up and she hugged me and made a kind of humming sound like she was singing to herself.

She is about two feet taller and a lot heavier than before. She is growing up fast. I feel like a proud poppa.

"Pure logical thinking cannot yield us any knowledge of the empirical world; all knowledge of reality starts from experience and ends in it. Propositions arrived at by purely logical means are completely empty of reality."

Albert Einstein

APPENDIX: Tips and cautions for long-term witnesses

If you suspect you have a Bigfoot in your backyard and wish to develop a relationship, please consider the following:

Apples are an ideal food to leave for the forest folks. They last a long time and are an indigenous food found all over the country.

Wash any store-bought fruit you leave out in order to remove as much pesticide residue as possible, and don't forget to remove the stickers.

Leave out plenty of food – remember: an apple is a mouthful for these guys. You wouldn't invite someone to dinner and give him one grape on his plate!

Stop thinking about these creatures as if they're some animal that you can outsmart. You can't. Treat them with the same respect that you would treat a tribe of aboriginal humans. They demand respect from one another… they're certainly going to expect it from you if you want to interact with them.

Do not, under ANY circumstances, shine infrared light in their face and think they can't see it. Don't shine a flashlight in their face. Their eyes are sensitive to light.

Don't assume that they're not watching you. Just because you can't see them, it doesn't mean they can't see you. They are masters at hiding, even in plain sight.

Be patient. Don't chase them. Let them come to you

Analyze your goals and intentions. Your behavior will reflect your agenda. If you go out and try to interact with these creatures with the intention of proving it to the world in the back of your mind, your behavior will reflect that and they will not trust you. If you want to gain their trust, *be trustworthy*.

Do not, under any circumstances, threaten a juvenile. They, like us, are intensely protective of their offspring.

While these creatures are cautious, but for the most part non-aggressive, remember that they are not bound by the social mores that require us to think before acting. They will ensure their survival and their survival often depends upon immediate, automatic reaction. If you threaten one, expect an IMMEDIATE response.

Treat them with respect. Treat them as INDIVIDUALS, not as an example of a species or a "specimen".

Be the first to end the encounter. Don't ask anything of them. Walk away. This is the most likely way to ensure another interaction.

Build trust. Be repetitive. Be consistent. Be PREDICATBLE.

Loud noises appear to frighten them. Don't "call-blast" or mimic their vocalizations in an attempt to "trick" them into answering, unless your goal is simply to record an irritated Sasquatch. If you're going to call to one of them, use your normal voice and call out as if you were calling to another person. Don't talk to them in a sticky-sweet tone of voice as if you're cajoling a skittish animal. Use a normal tone, keep it light, keep a sense of humor, and be matter-of-fact, calm and approachable.

Don't think you can outrun a Sasquatch. You can't.

A Sasquatch will not do anything it doesn't want to do. Remember this always.

Be cautious, but don't bother to look for Bigfoot if you can't keep a handle on your fear. People who are afraid often react to fear in a way that puts that which they fear in jeopardy. The more afraid you are, the more dangerous you are… and the more dangerous they will likely be. Frightened humans are the most dangerous creatures on this planet… and these guys know it.

Feel free to contact me if you're experiencing ongoing encounters and would like to discuss them with someone.

Finally… If you look for Bigfoot, don't be surprised if you find yourself in the process.

ABOUT THE AUTHOR

Autumn Williams lives in Oregon with her 3-year-old daughter, Rowan and her 13-year-old black kitty, Sabbath.

If you have had an experience with Bigfoot that you would like to share, you are encouraged to submit your report to the database at www.oregonbigfoot.com

You can also reach Autumn directly at info@oregonbigfoot.com

If you are a long-term witness, please consider coming forward and sharing your story. All personally identifying information, as well as the exact location of your sighting, will be kept strictly confidential upon request.